"If Joseph Heller's war began in 2004 instead of 1944, this would be *Catch-22*. I could not put the book down."

—*Seattle-Post Intelligencer*

"One diplomat's darkly humorous and ultimately scathing assault on just about everything the military and the State Department have done—or tried to do—since the invasion of Iraq. The title says it all."

—Steven Myers, *The New York Times*

"Long after the self-serving memoirs of people named Bush, Rice, and Rumsfeld are consigned to some landfill, this unsparing and very funny chronicle will remain on the short list of books essential to understanding America's Iraq War. Here is nation-building as it looks from the inside—waste, folly, and sheer silliness included."

—Andrew J. Bacevich, author of
Washington Rules: America's Path to Permanent War

"Laugh-out-loud funny . . . In more than 250 pages of text, Van Buren can think of almost no expenditure that made sense or helped with the long-term goal of stabilizing Iraq. Read it and weep, or laugh—or probably both."

—*The Dallas Morning News*

"A burn-his-bridges book by a foreign service officer . . . A scathing, gallows humor look at a massif of missteps . . . Van Buren is merciless."

—*The Boston Globe*

"An amusing or horrifying account of the disposition of $172 billion—depending on how sensitive one is to seeing U.S. taxpayer dollars seep into the Mesopotamian sand."

—*Pittsburgh Post-Gazette*

"Reality so rich it stuns. A time capsule, priceless deep insights into occupation at its worst."

—*Public Intelligence Blog*

"Checkbook diplomacy . . . In shopping for hearts and minds in Iraq, the State Department made some bizarre impulse purchases."

—*Foreign Policy*

"If this aint *Catch-22*, it's awfully close. *We Meant Well* is held together by Van Buren's hilariously rendered absurdities, from his encounters with American officials and their fictitious reconstruction projects to the U.S. command's annual distribution of a single can of beer to the troops. I laughed 'til I cried."

—*SpyTalk*

"A foreign service officer exposes the truth about American aid to Iraq, using satire, irony, and sometimes laugh-out-loud humor to convey grim reality."

—*The Kansas City Star*

"I've read just about every memoir out of Iraq and Afghanistan in the last decade, military or otherwise, and this stands as one of the best—certainly one of the most self-aware and best written."

—*Washingtonian*

"In this shocking and darkly hilarious exposé of the reconstruction of post-Saddam Iraq, former State Department team leader Van Buren describes the tragicomedy that has been American efforts at nation building, marked by bizarre decisions and wrongheaded priorities . . . With lyrical prose and biting wit, this book reveals the devastating arrogance of imperial ambition and folly."

—*Publishers Weekly* (Starred Review)

"The road to Hell is paved with taxpayer dollars in this insider's account of a misspent year rebuilding Iraq. Abrasive, honest, and funny."

—Nathan Hodge, author of
Armed Humanitarians: The Rise of the Nation Builders

"One of the rare, completely satisfying results of the expensive debacle in Iraq."

—*Kirkus Reviews* (Starred Review)

WE MEANT WELL

WE MEANT WELL

How I Helped

Lose the Battle

for the Hearts and Minds

of the Iraqi People

PETER VAN BUREN

Metropolitan Books • Henry Holt and Company • New York

Metropolitan Books
Henry Holt and Company, LLC
Publishers since 1866
175 Fifth Avenue
New York, New York 10010
www.henryholt.com

Metropolitan Books® and Ⓜ® are registered trademarks
of Henry Holt and Company, LLC.

Library of Congress Cataloging-in-Publication Data

Van Buren, Peter.
   We meant well : how I helped lose the war for the hearts and minds of the
Iraqi people / Peter Van Buren.
       p. cm.
   Includes bibliographical references.
   ISBN 978-0-8050-9681-1
   1. Postwar reconstruction—Iraq.   2. Iraq War, 2003—Public opinion.
3. United States—Relations—Iraq.   4. Iraq—Relations—United States.
5. Public opinion—Iraq.   I. Title.
   DS79.769.V36 2011
   956.7044'31—dc22

                                                        2011008821

Henry Holt books are available for special promotions and premiums.
For details contact: Director, Special Markets.

Originally published in hardcover in 2011 by Metropolitan Books

Designed by Meryl Sussman Levavi

Printed in the United States of America

D   10   9   8   7   6   5   4

For my lovely wife and family,

whom I missed terribly while in Iraq

Contents

WE MEANT WELL

My Arabic Library

About eighteen months before I arrived in Iraq, one of my predecessors had ordered My Arabic Library, $88,000 worth of books, an entire shipping container. My Arabic Library was a Bush-era, US government–wide project to translate classic American books, so we now have *Tom Sawyer, The House of the Seven Gables,* and *Of Mice and Men* in Arabic. The Embassy had big plans for the books, claiming, "It is so important that the children of Baghdad, the next generation of leaders of Iraq, obtain basic literacy skills. A love of learning and literacy will mean better job opportunities for them when they grow up. They will be able to better support their families and help build a more prosperous Iraq."[1]

Everyone forgot about the books until we learned that a truck was bringing them in from Jordan. After our prayers that the driver would abandon the truck en route failed, my team was stuck with the problem of what to do with a container of books that no one wanted. Apparently, there was little interest among Iraqi schools in reading *The Crucible* or *Moby-Dick,* as the books didn't fit into their centralized curriculum. I was charged with getting rid of them, to anywhere; the lucky winner needed only a truck. We cajoled a nearby school to take the whole mess from us as a personal favor. Their only condition was that they would not have to do the loading themselves, so that is how a couple of us ended up humping books into a flatbed truck while a high school principal and a local truck driver sat in the shade smoking, watching us. We heard later from a third party that, failing to sell the books on the black market, the principal just dumped them behind the school.

Help Wanted,
No Experience Necessary

The reconstruction of Iraq was the largest nation-building program in history, dwarfing in cost, size, and complexity even those undertaken after World War II to rebuild Germany and Japan. At a cost to the US taxpayer of over $63 billion and counting, the plan was lavishly funded, yet, as government inspectors found, the efforts were characterized from the beginning by pervasive waste and inefficiency, mistaken judgments, flawed policies, and structural weaknesses. Of those thousands of acts of waste and hundreds of mistaken judgments, some portion was made by me and the two reconstruction teams I led in Iraq, along with my goodwilled but overwhelmed and unprepared colleagues in the State Department, the military, and dozens of other US government agencies. We were the ones who famously helped paste together feathers year after year, hoping for a duck. The scholarly history someone will one day write about Iraq and reconstruction will need the raw material

of failure, and so this war story will try to explain how it all went
so wrong.

As a longtime Foreign Service Officer (FSO), I was sent by
the Department of State to Iraq for one year in 2009 as part of
the civilian Surge deployed to backstop the manlier military
one. Along with a half dozen contractors as teammates, I was
assigned to rebuild Iraq's essential services, to supply water and
sewer access as part of a counterinsurgency struggle to win
over the hearts and minds of the Iraqi people. It was Vietnam,
only better this time around, more T. E. Lawrence than Alden
Pyle. I was to create projects that would lift the local economy
and lure young men away from the dead-end opportunities of
al Qaeda. I was also to empower women, turning them into
entrepreneurs and handing them a future instead of a suicide
vest. A robust consumer society would do the trick, shopping
bags of affirmation leading to democracy.

Executing all this happiness required me to live with the
Army as part of an embedded Provincial Reconstruction Team
(ePRT) on a Forward Operating Base (FOB, rhymes with
"cob"). I spent the first six months on FOB Hammer in the
desert halfway between Baghdad and Iran before moving to
FOB Falcon just south of Baghdad for another half a year. In
the aftermath of the 2003 invasion, the United States established massive military bases throughout Iraq. Some, like the
grows-like-crabgrass Victory Base (the military has little sense
of irony), were as big as cities, with thousands of personnel, a
Burger King, samba clubs, Turkish hookah bars, and swimming pools. Some were much smaller, such as FOBs Hammer
and Falcon, with a couple of hundred soldiers each, Army food,
and portable latrines.

My work with the ePRTs involved traveling off the FOBs

to commute to the war. Unlike so-called fobbits, who spent most of their tour on base, I spent a lot of time outside the wire. I was to meet with Iraqis, hand them money for the projects we hoped would spring up, and then assess the results of our spending. Despite endless applications of money and violence prior to my arrival, the United States had failed to pacify Iraq, undertaking projects and holding elections in an endless loop of turning points and imagined progress. "Fuck 'em and feed 'em" was the cynical way it was referred to in Vietnam, dropping bombs at night on an area where we dropped food during the daylight hours, destroying history after dark and reconstructing it by day. In Iraq my predecessors evolved nicer ways of describing what we were trying to do, such as "counter-insurgency" or "civil capacity building." Regardless of the label, the one constant was that I could travel nowhere without an armored vehicle and armed soldiers for protection. Some of the soldiers on the FOB drove us around and pulled security for my team and me. The soldiers didn't seem to mind the task, as it was easy duty, albeit a bit boring, the day-to-day of imperial policing. We spent hours stuck in armored vehicles, a tedium that made golf seem like a contact sport, shared the futility of reconstructing things while they were still falling apart, and became close to one another in the intense but temporary way of relationships formed in war, like twelve months of one-night stands.

But I'm getting ahead of myself. This story really began in the early 1990s, as I sat ignorant in Taiwan processing tourist visas as a brand-new Foreign Service Officer while Saddam invaded Kuwait. Iraq had since then been continuously under siege by the United States. During Desert Storm we destroyed large portions of its infrastructure. We had gone out of our way to make a mess, using clever tools such as cruise missiles that spat metallic fibers to short out entire electrical systems we would have to reconstruct. In the years that followed Desert Storm, three US Presidents bombed and rocketed Iraq, running up the bill we would later have to pay. Sanctions meanwhile kept Saddam fat and happy on black-market oil profits while chiseling away Baghdad's cosmopolitan First World veneer and plunging most of Iraq's population into poverty. Events in Iraq ebbed and flowed through the US media over the years but the storm never ended for most Iraqis. It was a seamless epic as the war of 1990–91 continued through the no-fly zones and the sanctions of the nineties, to be capped off by the 2003 invasion and the ensuing years of occupation.

The script for the 2003 invasion did not include an extended reconstruction effort. It instead imagined Americans being greeted as liberators like in post-D-day France, with cheerful natives rushing out to offer our spunky troops bottles of wine and frisky daughters. The Bush administration ignored the somber prewar predictions of the State Department, cut it out of the immediate postwar process, and instead whipped together a blended family of loyal interns, contractors, and soldiers to witness the complete implosion of Iraqi civil society. Things got steadily worse in Iraq as the early Coalition Provisional Authority and military efforts at reconstruction failed, the UN was bypassed, and the security situation discouraged even the hardiest NGOs. By about 2005, the White House saw the need to kick the war into higher gear, sending in the increased deployment of troops known as the Surge, while the Pentagon dusted off the old books from Vietnam for tips on counterinsurgency philosophy. There was originally in the military about as much enthusiasm for reviving counterinsurgency as there might have been for reinstating horse-borne cavalry charges and cutlasses. We were back in a Vietnam kind of war. It wasn't enough just to kill people and destroy villages. We had to win over the ones still alive, get them to adopt a democratic system and become our allies. Victory would be ours not when we pacified Iraq militarily but when the country was stable enough to stand on its own. This was counterinsurgency, hearts and minds, soft power, whatever you wanted to call it. In the improvisational spirit of the whole war, it was decided that the State Department had better get involved in a big way. State would rebuild and reconstruct Iraq, win over the people with democracy, and then we could all pack up for home.

The vehicle for these accomplishments would be State Department–led Provincial Reconstruction Teams like the ones I served on. PRTs harkened back to the failed Civil Operations and Rural Development Support (CORDS) program in Vietnam, in which State, the US Agency for International Development (USAID), and military personnel theoretically worked together to improve the lives of local people and so distance them from the insurgents. In practical terms, PRTs were locally located State Department outposts, usually in or near big cities like Baghdad, Mosul, and Erbil. The first PRT popped up in Baghdad in the spring of 2006. The Secretary of State herself flew in for one of the grand openings in Mosul. At the peak in 2007, there were thirty-one PRTs and thirteen ePRTs in Iraq, a few run by stalwart allies like South Korea and the British.[2] (Unlike an ePRT, which lived tightly enmeshed with the military, a regular PRT stood apart from the military, with its own contracted mercenary security.) By 2009, the Provincial Reconstruction Teams had shrunk in number to sixteen and were All-American, though a former Italian journalist still headed the one in Dhi Qar, where they had a wood-burning pizza oven and enjoyed red wine with dinner, no doubt easing the strain of war. The teams would leave Iraq after the soldiers did, this time the mission truly accomplished.

The Department of State wanted a lot from its reconstruction teams, as expressed in its vision statement.[3] The teams were "aligned with" the key US priority of:

> . . . promoting stability and development at the provincial level to support a sovereign, stable and self-reliant Iraq that is integrated into the global economy. By assisting Iraqis in strengthening the capacity of their government institutions and civil society, the PRTs deepen coopera- tion at the local level, build stronger relationships, encour- age economic diversification and foreign investment, foster the development of transparent and accountable gover- nance, promote rule of law, confront corruption, deliver essential public services, improve public health and pro- mote stability and community development.

But saying so couldn't make it true. The whole of reconstruc- tion was plagued by problems from the start.

For the first years of the war, the military had run recon- struction on its own, albeit haphazardly. The Army conceptu- alized the work as doing a few favors for the locals, such as vaccinating farm animals or handing out candy, enough to tame the wilderness. State had a much bigger mandate, nothing less than raising up an economically sound, democratic Iraq. The differences in mission and approach would dog the PRT program for its entire sad life.

Complicating matters was that the reconstruction effort was fragmented and understaffed. By July 2007, sixty-two US government agencies were involved in the project. When General David Petraeus took over the war in Iraq, his advisers identified eight major coordination bodies at the Embassy in Baghdad. "We have an underdeveloped Iraqi bureaucracy and an overdeveloped US bureaucracy," one Petraeus adviser observed. On the ground we were spread far too thin for so daunting a mission. The East Rasheed ePRT, for example, had to serve a population the size of Detroit with a staff of six. The ePRT in southern Baghdad had eight people from State embedded with 3,700 soldiers tending to one million Iraqis.

Raw number of personnel aside, properly staffing the PRTs and ePRTs with the right mix of people proved to be the greatest challenge of all. The Department of State struggled to field adequate numbers of qualified employees from among its own ranks, forcing the creation of an army of contractors, called 3161s after the name of the legislation in 5 USC 3161 that created their hiring program. They were supposed to be SMEs (pronounced smee, not s-m-e), subject matter experts, a term that became a part of the war's large lexicon of ironic phrases. "Iraq is not for amateurs," said Ambassador Chris Hill in Baghdad, though it was mostly amateurs whom the State Department found.[4] The main criterion for hiring seemed to be an interest in living in Iraq for a year with a $250,000 salary and three paid vacations, and so that took a front seat to any actual skills. In the enthusiasm to staff up, most of these people were hired without interviews, directly off their often wobbly résumés.

Though some of the 3161s turned out to be talented, it was more by luck, personal pluck, or accident than by design. State assigned people roles based on merit badges earned: a former local council member became a senior governance adviser, while a female gym teacher from the Midwest morphed into a women's empowerment programmer. Imagine the old Andy Hardy movies, where the kids' enthusiasm was supposed to make up for the lack of costumes and props.

The need for 3161s to live on a military base also skewed hiring toward former military, nearly self-defeating the idea of providing a civilian side to the reconstruction. The Office of the Special Inspector General for Iraq Reconstruction (SIGIR) in its review of the PRTs' first year of operation found an Army veterinarian developing agriculture programs, an aviation maintenance manager as a PRT coleader, and advisers to Iraqi provincial governors who included a former Navy submariner, an ultrasound technician, and a Drill Sergeant. PRTs were short of personnel who could best assist Iraqis in developing the capacity to administer the economy, establish the rule of law, and foster good governance, often because the 3161s didn't know how to do these things either. Language was also a problem, as almost none of the 3161s spoke any Arabic. As the State Department did not provide language training, the grand total of Arabic speakers among the 610 PRT personnel deployed in mid-2007 was 29.

Added to the mix were a few genuine State Department FSOs. The first wave was a rare bunch, folks interested in adventure, danger junkies, a few serious Arabists eager to try out their skills. However, with only several thousand FSOs worldwide (even today there are more military band members than FSOs) and embassies and consulates to staff all around the world, State quickly ran out of the relatively small pool of happy few volunteers. What to do?

The Vietnam CORDS program was the last time the Department of State "directed" Foreign Service Officers into positions abroad that they did not want to take. The program's name was invoked in whispered conversations all over Foggy Bottom as the Department tried to drum up the next wave of volunteers for Iraq. A small minority of FSOs objected politically to doing anything to support the Bush wars of choice, but really, most of us were just unsure of our role, untrained in how to survive in war, and unclear what the point was anyway. FSOs thus initially stayed away. For political reasons, Secretary of State Condoleezza Rice was loath to ask Congress for additional, new Foreign Service Officer positions. With the volunteer pool empty and no new FSOs forthcoming that could be tasked to Iraq, all that was left was option number three, to deploy a carrot and stick against existing personnel. This is where I came in.

My side of State was removed from the high-level WikiLeaky things ambassadors did and changed very little between administrations. We worked with Americans who were victims of crime abroad, helping them get home. We took care of folks who got arrested and evacuated people caught up in earthquakes and coups. This was the benign side of empire, the ability to care for our citizens pretty much anywhere in the world. Despite the enthusiasm for the new PRT idea at the higher levels, the rank and file of the State Department like me were unsure if this was right for us. We were ready to hop in after the shooting was over but would do what we could to avoid a fight. Yes, 9/11 had changed everything, we'd heard that, but the concept of inserting us into the middle of a war did not sit well.

Things got serious after State changed personnel rules to make it nearly impossible to get promoted without an Iraq (or Afghanistan, now also Pakistan) tour and added some financial incentives such as special danger pay. With these carrots and sticks, discord was tamped down, the conservative pundits were put back in their cages (Michelle Malkin in particular suggested someone should slap the "weenie and whiner FSOs" who refused to serve in Iraq), and the FSOs were lined up for the surging PRT program without anyone's having to be forced to go, sort of.[5]

I had never served in the Middle East and knew nothing about rebuilding past the Home Depot guides, but people like me were what the Department had been dealt to play this game. The new rules boxed me into serving or seeing my career flatline. Less cynically, despite my reservations about the war, I still believed in the idea of service (love the warrior, hate the war) and wanted to test myself. I also needed the money, and so the nexus of duty, honor, terrorism, and my oldest daughter's college tuition (hopefully there'll be another war when my youngest is college age) led another FSO into semivoluntarily joining The Cause. Between war and peace lies reconstruction and I would try to do my part.

But first, training, or so I thought. Despite the enormity of our task and the stated importance to the interests of the United States, preparation for PRT duty was amazingly brief, all of three weeks. Week One was five days of what we called Islam for Dummies, a quick overview of the religion with some pointers on "Arab" culture (dudes kiss, no serving bacon, no joking about God). Some mention of Sunnis and Shias was made but the conflict came off more like a sports rivalry than open warfare. The instructor was former military and sounded a lot like Dr. Phil, which was very comforting. It felt like we would be holding an intervention for the war, forcing it to confront its shortcomings—"Tell him, tell him to his face, you are a bad war. You disappointed me, war." Dr. Phil also gave us our only Arabic language training, ninety minutes of handy phrases and greetings.

Week Two was an overview of the simple spreadsheets and database we'd use to track millions of dollars of project grants, plus a negotiating session where a local Iraqi American was called in to pretend to be a town mayor. He asked for a bribe and then gave me permission to build a dam (in Iraq I never built any dams and there were no mayors in the small towns I visited). Since the class included both longtime State employees and our new contractor colleagues, we all sat politely through a dreary session on how an embassy works. Since there was nothing Middle Eastern in the neighborhood, the class went out as a group to lunch at a Chinese restaurant. Really good pork buns.

Week Three took place at an undisclosed location in West Virginia where we learned defensive driving skills (none of us ever drove on the streets of Iraq) and had a weapons familiarization course (all FSOs in Iraq were unarmed). The last time I punched someone was in junior high school. I was never in the military. I had at that moment never fired a weapon. A Real Man with a biker beard, angry tats, an NYPD baseball cap, and serious sunglasses loaded a weapon (I called them guns then) and carefully placed it in my hands. He kept his own veined, masculine paws on the cold steel, helped me aim it at a very nearby target, and then told me to pull the trigger. He did this for our group of about twenty-five State Department employees.

After each shot, without looking at the target or the shooter, the Man said, "Hit, good shot," and took the weapon back to prepare for the next person.

After only fifteen school days I was fully trained to lead an ePRT in the midst of a shooting war. Missing from the training was any history of the war and our policy, any review of past or current reconstruction projects, any information on military organization, acronyms, and rank structure, any lessons learned from the previous years' work, or any idea of what the hell a PRT was and what our job was going to be. They never told us anything about what we were supposed to do once we got there. What we did get was a firm handshake from Dr. Phil and a ride to the airport. I was off to Iraq.

Inhaling: Arriving in Iraq

I showed up at the airport with an absurd amount of luggage, not knowing what to take to a war. The clerk at the counter saw my new boots and one-way ticket to Kuwait and helpfully asked, "Are you a soldier?" She quickly explained that soldiers do not have to pay to check extra luggage. I stammered out a "yes" to save some money, leaving for later the philosophical questions of who exactly it was that was going to Iraq and whether I could truthfully claim to be fighting for my country.

We landed with a thump in the dusky Kuwaiti evening fourteen hours later. I was ass deep in this now, with a feeling of inevitability that was uncomfortable, unfamiliar, overwhelming. At the same time, the inevitability was cathartic, sort of the way fear dissipates just after you jump off the high board. I did not know them then, but all around me were the people I would live with for a year in Iraq: the carpetbaggers, the Iraqi American prospectors, the tired divorced contractors making

$250K a year, the odd soldier coming back from emergency leave, the newbies trying to look old, the burned-out third timers, the Third World slavers, and the mad, mad young ones desperate to burn off their youth in an adventure that would likely not end well. This was not something you got into, it was something you ended up in. Some may have been on their first trip abroad, others held golden frequent-flier status such that they were practically allowed to pilot the plane if they wished. I wanted the air to feel electric and for people to ask me who I was and why I was there, but the air was dry and nobody cared who else was present—a crowd of the lost milling toward a sad guy whose job it was to hold a cardboard sign telling us where to go next. Unlike the military, who deployed by unit, we walked in, and later out, alone.

I was scooped up by people working for Kellogg Brown and Root (KBR), the mega contracting firm connected to Dick Cheney's Halliburton. KBR's Kuwait staff were big-bellied crackers wearing sports team ball caps, blue jeans with belts and suspenders, all fat as Shetland ponies. The Clampetts had occupied Kuwait. They walked around the airport looking for fresh meat, me, like lumpy islands in a smooth sea of wealthy, perfumed Kuwaitis in their white man dresses and headgear. KBR had created a fiercely huge but inefficient organism to process us into Iraq. The task seemed simple: move us passengers from the commercial airport to the US Air Force base hidden in the Kuwaiti desert so we could get on a military flight to Baghdad. The base was a legacy from when the United States invaded Kuwait after chasing out the invading Iraqis in 1991. We followed the KBR guy like ducklings, dragging luggage as part of the parade. We gathered at the immigration counter, split up, reassembled on the other side, and gathered and split for processing a few more times until we were outside in the dark, waiting for a line of Econoline vans. The van ride was forty-five minutes in darkness, the only noise the squalling radio the KBR driver used to shout things like "Departing!" and "On Route Tampa!" at a volume that made me think he did not understand what the radio part did and was trying to make his voice carry.

If I had been able to sleep I would have jerked awake when the van stopped. It was seriously black dark, and while I generally knew what time the plane had landed, there was no way to tell what time it really was anymore. I stumbled off the van with everyone else, amazed to see ground under my feet. I scuffed sand on my boots so they looked less new (they still looked new). The KBR guys herded us into a huge hangar that might have been purgatory, if God drove a Greyhound. Hundreds of beaten-down recliner chairs lined up as if facing a distant screen, with the ambience of a bowling alley snack bar. Soldiers, civilians, and probably actual gypsies were sleeping or sitting upright, staring at nothing. The place smelled of sweat and sand. Cletus moved us from station to station, each pause accomplishing something small I did not understand—hand over ID card, get it back, walk over there and fill out a form, walk somewhere else and repeat 90 percent of the process, everything done by hand, on paper. I was thrown a helmet and body armor ripe with someone else's sweat, black and greasy at the collar, wrote my name on a piece of duct tape, and stuck it to my chest as told, and then, suddenly, it was time to wait.

After what seemed like a week but was only two hours, we were led again through an obstacle course of counters and clipboards and onto a bus. Eventually we got to a runway and marched into the belly of a C-130 cargo aircraft fitted with facing rows of canvas sling seats as if to pretend we weren't really just more cargo. The aircraft warming up was noisy, while the aircrew shouted silently, their voices drowned out. We sat with our legs interwoven, helmets and body armor on, in near-complete darkness as the plane took off.

I must have fallen asleep, because the thump as the plane landed woke me from a warm bed far away. A crew member said simply, "Baghdad." Outside I looked at the concrete and smelled the aviation fuel, trying to have a significant moment, until someone pushed me and I joined a long line that led to another line, where I showed more people the same ID card. By the time my wife was ready to give birth, after a thousand examinations, she'd simply stopped caring who saw her naked, and I now felt the same way, waving my card at complete strangers on the assumption that they wanted to see it. We wrote our names on lists and more lists. There must be a thousand clipboards at the Baghdad airport. I did not know why I was getting on another bus or where I was going. I wanted to sleep, I wanted to get rid of my luggage, and I wanted to ask so many questions.

The bus was sucked down tunnels made of concrete T-walls. Everything was brightly lit with the uncaring orange glow you see on the interstate late at night. We did the ID mambo again and again, even onboard until someone said to get off the bus. I asked everyone I could where we were and got multiple answers. It turned out we were (by summation) in Iraq, Baghdad, Victory Base Complex, Camp Stryker, at the Rhino Stables. The Stables were filled with old furniture and a million paperbacks left by others—this was a place for serious waiting. One of our legacies in Iraq will be the mountains of murder mystery, sci-fi, romance, and fantasy paperbacks left behind to confound future archaeologists. There was a TV with CNN and another with sports, the sound turned off on both, Anderson Cooper as mime. Handwritten signs were everywhere: take one, replace one, eat what you take, no feet on couches, no smoking, check your weapon, official calls only, one per customer, keep quiet when others are sleeping, no sleeping on couches. It felt temporarily permanent, a place that was never meant to exist for too long but that had accepted its new fate without even a feint at grace. I asked at the desk what I was waiting for, and the person there, with yellow-brown teeth chronicling a lifetime of unfiltered Camels, told me I was waiting for the Rhino, so sit down. If I could have, I would have willed myself to spontaneously combust and be done with all this. If anyone had said, "We're not in Kansas anymore, Toto," I would have torn off his limbs and beaten his torso to a pulp with a leg.

At some point late in the night, time ceased to matter. A worker yelled that the Rhino had arrived. A soldier tore the duct tape off my vest without asking, saying it made me look "new," and I hated and thanked him at the same time. The Rhino turned out to be an armored bus, with thick windows and a Thunderdome feel. Inside it felt darker than the night because the windows were tinted. The guard onboard told us to put on our helmets because "we're gonna enter Iraq soon." I was scared, and I was suddenly very, very awake. My neck started to sweat even though the bus was cold. I wanted to be anywhere else. I was willing to go back to the La-Z-Boys in Kuwait. I stayed hyperalert the entire one-hour ride, aware of every bump and turn. My vision blurred and my mouth was cotton-dry. I had no control, I felt stupid being frightened, I wanted to go home.

It was unclear to me in my state when exactly we left Iraq and entered the Green Zone and, soon after that, the Embassy compound. Someone handed me a key and pointed me toward a dorm door, told me to be outside at 8:00 a.m., and left. I found my room, my clothing soaked clean through in frigid sweat. I had to get up in a few hours to be helicoptered to my new home in the desert. Unable to sleep, I turned on the TV. The first channel to pop up showed a *Seinfeld* rerun in English and I watched that until three. I hate that bass-riff thing *Seinfeld* uses to bridge between scenes, but no one was around to listen or care.

A Home in the Desert

From high up in the air my new home looked like a ship, a speck floating in the sea of Iraq, affected by it but not part of it. For the next six months, I would live at this place, FOB Hammer, embedded first with the 82nd Airborne Division, followed by the 10th Mountain Division, two of the Army's proudest can-do units. FOB Hammer was purpose-built in 2007 for the Surge, and it sat out in the literal middle of nowhere. I say literal, literally, because there was no town or feature, man-made or natural, to mark it or lend it a name. It was its own kingdom, built entirely by the US Army to house the US Army. They simply picked a flat piece of ground and moved in, with the squatter's rights a successful invasion granted. FOB Hammer was physically huge, twelve miles around its perimeter, and surrounded by rings of ubiquitous T-walls, cast concrete twelve feet high with a wide base so they could stand on their own. T-walls were as iconic to our war as Betty Grable was to that other, better war. The walls kept us in our ship and they kept Iraq out. As a hint there was something more out there, I smelled wood fires burning as we landed. Someone explained Iraqis used scraps of palm wood for fuel. It was a very old thing to do. There was not much fuel in the desert, and people throughout the Middle East had burned palm wood for millennia. Jesus smelled palm wood burning.

The FOB was subdivided into parts of town where one spent a lot of time and parts where one did not venture, all populated by about four hundred troops. A few places, like where the helicopters touched down or the single land gate in and out, were necessary stops but otherwise to be avoided. The landing zone (LZ) was way out on the edge of the FOB, presumably for safety (if a helo crashed it was better somewhere unpopulated). People went to the LZ to get on and off birds; there were a lot of cigarette butts on the ground but otherwise it was distant, noisy, dangerous, and without amenities.

The gate was a bad place to hang out because you could be shot. The gate was not a front door like at Fort Apache but rather a series of stages that transitioned you from outside to inside. The journey in started with the dirt road that led to Hammer. The road acquired barbed wire as it approached the FOB, followed by concrete barriers that forced vehicles to slow down and execute a series of S-turns, followed by the first line of Hesco barriers. (Made by the Hesco company, whose stock you should have bought in 2002, these gigantic wire baskets, taller than a person, were lined with waterproof cardboard and filled with dirt to make thick walls.) A flat area, the "kill zone," filled with razor wire and watched over by contracted guards in medieval-looking concrete towers, was the final defense. Unless you were going out on patrol, people tended to fly in and out of the FOB for safety and because it was so damn far away from the world. The twenty-first century did not bring me a personal portable jetpack or a hoverboard, but I did get to travel a lot by helicopter while in Iraq.

Once past the gate and another series of S-turns designed to slow down suicide bombers and piss off tired soldiers, the road in brought you to the center part of the FOB, where almost all of us lived amid a series of abbreviations and acronyms. Despite wildly varying rank, duties, and salary, everyone shared the same life. Soldiers, contractors, and I all lived in the same trailers, ate the same food, used the same showers. The military term for this zone was LSA (life support area), which translated to air-conditioned trailers (called CHUs, for containerized housing units) and a chow hall called a DFAC (dining facility), a gym (GYM), an MWR (morale, welfare, and recreation) Internet room with VoIP phones (Voice over Internet Protocol) and satellite AFN TV (Armed Forces Network), a tiny PX (post exchange), and maybe a fast-food trailer. A proper LSA was an outpost of the homeland. It affirmed morale. Even the postboxes were blue and imported from the States. It was supposed to look like home and it sort of did, if home was a trailer park and Taco Bell was a night out.

The CHUs where we all lived were steel containers modified to become little rooms. Most people insisted on calling them hooches, invoking the 'Nam slang term, but it was hard for me to think of my steel box as anything as exotic as what the term *hooch* called up. The box was as long as a single bed plus three feet and just wider than my extended arms. Inside you had one or two beds, one or two IKEA-like freestanding closets, and as much junk as you and your roommate could cram in. During the times when I was lucky enough to live alone I kept the place fairly empty, but some soldiers acquired a frightening amount of what was technically known as crap, piling Xboxes (the value of video games to the war should not be undersold; troops would finish work patrolling the streets of 2010 Iraq to play *Call of Duty*, patrolling the streets of 1945 Berlin), cheap TVs, hundreds of DVDs, boom boxes, exercise gear, and stolen snack foods, pyramided from floor to ceiling. Everybody had to cram in their weapons and ammunition. The soldiers also had to deploy with all their issued gear, needed or not, so their hooches would also be piled high with cold-weather gear, bulky rubber chemical-protection suits, and arctic sleeping bags. There'd be regular inspections for forbidden drugs, booze, and any temporary cohabiting, and those rude checkups when everything was tossed around kept most hooches in a state of near collapse.

Like most everything else on the FOB, our offices were temporary things. The Army had built a large building, about the size of a high school gym, and created within it a warren of rooms and cubicles and dead ends without cheese, all made out of plywood sheets. It was meant to be temporary (we're not occupiers, you know!) but like a Big Mac left on a shelf it never rotted away. Nothing was painted, because paint was an enhancement, not a requirement, and so we had no paint inside. Outside rocks were painted white to make moving around at night easier, so there paint was a necessity and permitted. My office was decorated only by giant maps of Iraq and by dust.

I had two old laptops, one for classified and one for unclassified. Unfortunately, I had only one power adapter, and so throughout the day I had to switch the power between machines as one battery or the other faded out. There was no legitimate method to procure a second power adapter, so I had to either buy one myself and wait eight weeks for it to arrive by military mail from Dell or steal one when someone transferred off the FOB. Furniture was a similar problem. Sometime before I arrived in Iraq, the ePRT had been relocated from FOB Loyalty to FOB Hammer. All of our office furniture had been lost in the move. State insisted that under some obscure memorandum of understanding the Army was responsible for furnishing our office. After doing so, the Army felt that even if it then stole the furniture for its own use, it was under no obligation to give us new furniture. While this was worked out at high levels, we used sheets of plywood for desks and sat on crates. The same problem came up with printer cartridges; State said they were a DOD responsibility and DOD said State should pay. For a while we couldn't print anything in our office and had to beg permission to print from neighbors until an unnamed person stole some printer cartridges from the Embassy for us.

The few Iraqis allowed on the FOB ran shops, created as part of a long-forgotten program to nurture small business in Iraq. The soldiers to a man and woman called these "hajji shops," misappropriating the formal Islamic term for a devout Muslim who has made the pilgrimage to Mecca. *Hajji* used in this fashion was this war's kraut, Jap, and gook. The shops sold mostly office supplies (but not printer cartridges) and illegal DVDs. The office supplies were popular because the Army supply chain could be slow and seemed always to be out of what you needed. It was easier to buy yellow stickies for a few dollars than to order them through the Army. We believed many of the office supplies in the hajji shops were stolen from the Army, which was one reason the Army was usually out of what you needed.

Illegal DVDs constituted about 90 percent of the hajji

shops' inventory and close to 100 percent of their profits. The DVDs were an encyclopedic collection of action, adventure, and car-chase movies from the birth of cinema to the most recent *Fast and Furious*. The DVDs all came from China. One can only imagine the reverse Silk Road journey these movies made from a back-alley copying operation in Guangzhou to a hajji shop at the FOB. All that and you could get a movie for three bucks. After oil, it seemed like illegal DVD sales made up the other half of the Iraqi economy. Some soldiers had collections of hundreds.

Near the semiofficial hajji shops were the official franchises, sponsored by the Army and Air Forces Exchange Service (AAFES). These shops existed on almost every FOB of decent size. They included a barbershop, an out-of-place embroidery shop (almost all name tapes and rank badges were now stuck on uniforms with Velcro), and a fake fast-food stand (sign says Pizza Hut, food says generic frozen). Then there was the PX, a cross between a general store and a gas station convenience shop. It didn't have much but it had the necessities. Soldiers could buy toiletries, three-month-old magazines, batteries, a few music CDs (the rack would have three rap artists, three country artists, and three heavy metal groups, all about a year out of style, to displease everyone equally), and lonely full-price versions of some of the same DVDs the hajji shops sold.

The bad side of town was the semianonymous area where the Ugandan contract guards and Third World servants who cleaned the latrines and served the food stayed. They lived in tents while we lived in trailers, and their tents were one of the places on the FOB where you did not go. I envisioned the area as a dust bowl hobo camp. They were so removed from us that if someone told me the FOB had secret utilidoor tunnels underneath like Disney World, I would have believed it too. At the Embassy, I knew they lived crammed into unsafe shipping containers, with all sorts of fire hazards.[6] We often wondered what their lives were like, if they ever did things for fun, and how many hours they worked. There were rumors, too, about the Ugandan camp, that drugs were available and that two rapes had occurred there. No one knew what was true, but we all kept away.

Our area of responsibility was the Maadain, a loosely defined rural area that used to be Iraq's breadbasket but was now a Sunni-Shia battleground centered on the town of Salman Pak. My ePRT teammates had abandoned FOB Hammer long before I arrived as being too distant from where they were running most of our projects. One teammate hung on alone at another FOB while the others moved into Cache South. Named after a hospital that was no longer there, Cache South actually sat on top of the former Iraqi nuclear reactor site, the one bombed by the Israelis in the 1980s even before the United States began its own wars against Iraq. Cache South was simply a bunch of hooches stuck between giant sand berms that originally protected the nuke site against everything but Israeli airplanes overhead. Fewer than one hundred soldiers, plus my teammates, lived at South. It was a helicopter ride away, and I was scheduled to visit it in the very near future. I planned to look there for laptop power adapters and printer cartridges.

With the offices, shops, and living areas clustered in the center, FOB Hammer had a lot of open spaces around the inside of its perimeter. The extra land was to allow for future expansion or just to create more of a security buffer between the exterior walls and where most of the people were. Way out on the edge of FOB Hammer were several small hills, lumps of raised dirt on the otherwise frying-pan-flat desert. These were "tells," ancient garbage dumps and fallen buildings. Thousands of years ago, people in this area used sun-dried bricks to build homes and walls. The sun-dried bricks lasted about twenty years before crumbling, at which point the people rebuilt on top of the old foundation. After a couple of rounds, the buildings sat on a small hill. There had been so much erosion over the years, along with the digging the Army had done, that an entire area two football fields in size was covered with pottery shards. In a few minutes of wandering around, I found pieces commingled that were handworked (old), spun on a wheel with grooves (less old), and glazed with blue color (newest). People said that when the Army first built the FOB and dug up truckloads of dirt, they found skulls and long bones. You could sometimes spot very old bones in the dirt inside the Hesco barriers. (The Army used one ancient hill for artillery practice, blowing off most of the top. As one soldier said, "If it's old and already broken, why does it matter if we shoot at it?") The Army digging also exposed an old village perimeter wall, short-lasting sun-dried bricks on the bottom with a row or two of longer-lasting kiln-dried bricks on top for sturdiness. There was little wood in the desert for kilns, so the inhabitants could not build the whole wall out of the sturdier brick. There was still a large brick factory in the area, a few miles from the FOB, that made bricks with local mud. With only a little water added, the mud turned thick and sticky, bad for walking, great for bricks.

Some ten thousand tells are scattered all over the Middle East. You could see them in the desert from the helicopter, especially in the late afternoon when the sun was low, as they were the only things that cast a significant shadow. An ancient river once flowed through this area, with the village adjacent.

A band of greenery marked where the river had been, suggesting there was still water deep underneath. Some of the pottery and bricks were likely Sumerian. It was possible the dust I dug out of my ears at night might have been part of an ancient wall around a Sumerian city. At night the tell area was very dark so as to avoid giving the insurgents an easy aiming point, and you could imagine how the earliest inhabitants of what was now FOB Hammer must have seen the night sky. It was a reminder that we were not the first to move into Iraq from afar, and a promise across time that someone might sit atop our own ruins and wonder whatever happened to the Americans.

Not all bases were conjured up out of nothing, appearing one day fully formed in the middle of the desert. The second place I lived, embedded with the 3rd Infantry Division, was FOB Falcon. Located on the edge of urban Baghdad, Falcon was convenient to our area of responsibility in what used to be called the "Sunni Triangle of Death" (Army and Embassy PR people ordered the term embargoed once they wanted us to seem like we were winning). Starting with the southern border of Baghdad city proper, the area spread like spilled paint east into Rasheed and Doura and south toward Mahmudiyah. FOB Falcon was a cement factory before the Army arrived uninvited in 2003. They took it because they needed it, and they had won the war that month. They sometimes forgot that the things they appropriated had belonged to someone else, to the point where the Army held elaborate ceremonies to "gift" the places back to ungrateful Iraqis after they were done with them.

FOB Falcon was something from a *Mad Max* movie, run-down, apocalyptic. Next door was a vast open field five times the size of a Walmart parking lot, filled with rusted old vehicles. The contractors hired to haul away our American garbage had a quicker turnaround when they dumped it nearby, and so these flats outside the wire were covered in trash, picked over by the Iraqis, who fought with feral dogs and scavenger birds for the good stuff. The assembled houses of the Iraqis were funny-sad caricatures of us, with Hesco baskets framing walls and large discarded placards reading "Deadly Force Authorized" as roofs. Old office chairs lined up around many of the houses and corrugated tin walls corralled tired goats and mean dogs.

On the FOB itself, the Army cleaned things up like teenagers tidied their rooms, pushing refuse aside only enough to make room for new stuff. They always seemed to leave pieces from the previous life of the place to remind you that it used to be something else, and in the case of Falcon it was a garish flagpole base in turquoise tile with faux gold trim, in the style of designer excess that the Iraqi elite seemed to favor. Otherwise, the cement factory warehouse became the Army warehouse, the cement factory office became the Army office, and so forth. Though it was more urban and smaller than Hammer, Falcon and every other FOB in Iraq was really just more of the same, the LSA, the hooches, the DFAC, all the same stuff, as if the FOBs were built as franchises.

Three things distinguished FOB Falcon. One was that it had its own unmanned observation blimp, a huge blob that floated overhead festooned with cameras and electronics and sensors to allow it to monitor the base and the surrounding area. With the appropriate clearance, you could watch the video feed from your desktop computer as the soldier in charge zoomed in on patches of real life outside our walls. In the odd way that soldiers entertained themselves, dogs going at it were always worth zooming in on, and one troop claimed to have a night-vision-enhanced video clip that will never make WikiLeaks, showing a man in close carnality with a donkey. The eye in the sky blimp caught the morning and evening light turning pink, red, and purple at different times and adding something almost aesthetic to the neighborhood.

Falcon also had decent cable TV, only $25 a month, provided by local Iraqis. They supplied pirated CNN, BBC, and a bunch of channels ripped off from Dubai satellites that played American TV shows (*Survivor* reruns in English and *The Simpsons* in Arabic). Installation involved the guys punching a hole in your hooch wall with a sharpened screwdriver and dropping the cable through to mate with your TV. Cable was run from hooch to hooch, so if a neighbor pulled out the wire everyone downstream of him went black.

Falcon's other distinguishing feature was a serious mud-brick wall wrapped around its perimeter, left over from when the same wall protected the cement factory. Rather than tearing the wall down or fixing it up, the Army just strung razor wire along the top while building another wall inside, with towers and standing places that would not have looked odd to the Sumerian archers who had once most certainly populated this area, their remains still being dug up in the desert.

Unexpected Blows:
Day One with My Team

If this were a movie, the opening scenes would present me as a somewhat bright-eyed, wisecracking, reasonably enthusiastic war agnostic ready to go to work in Iraq. By act two I would start to see the cracks in our approach in Iraq, only to end the film bitter and disillusioned. The reality for me in Iraq was more like falling off a cliff. In perhaps a slightly different context, though still in our neighborhood, the prophet Isaiah quotes Allah as saying "their words are meaningless, and their hearts are somewhere else. . . . So I will startle them with one unexpected blow after another." Helicoptering out of Hammer to meet my teammates at their even more austere location at Cache South, I was off to my first day of work with my ePRT. The unexpected blows came one after another.

The morning started with a staff postmortem on a previous week's conference for local area NGOs. Held at a Green Zone hotel, the conference had devolved into a shouting match between Kurdish sympathizers and everyone else present. The conference organizer, an Iraqi nicknamed McBlazer because he had adopted the State Department "field uniform" of blue blazer with khakis, now sought an additional $3,250 because supposedly more people showed up than anticipated. My brand-new coworkers Mel, Robert, James, and Michael asked me if I would approve the extra money for McBlazer. I said no, as he had agreed to a contract. McBlazer's original bid had included an outrageous $52 a head for printing. Robert explained that because of funding restrictions on meals, McBlazer had hidden some of the food costs in the printing costs. This was "normal." No one could explain the odd discrepancies between the number of guests and the costs (on the bid sheets 280 guests cost more than 300 guests). Worse, McBlazer insisted there had in fact been 280 guests even though the official count was only 206. McBlazer's request for additional money made no sense, except as a shakedown.

This sparked an animated discussion, during which James accused me of calling everyone dishonest for hiding meal costs inside fake printing receipts. James spat that relationships were the most important thing in Iraq and if I muddied them my time as ePRT team leader would not last long. Mel protested that McBlazer was an important partner we had to "take care of" and admonished me not to make our first interaction a problematic one by being honest. Robert barked that I needed to learn to work well with others before pounding that table. Michael worried that without McBlazer we would not be able to hold future conferences and that McBlazer had threatened to withdraw his services from other ePRTs at a time when the Embassy was gung ho on big conferences. I would be responsible for an Iraq-wide breakdown on my first day. McBlazer, Mel whispered, had married into a powerful Kurdish political family, and we needed to pay him off for our safety.

If I were describing this experience in a novel, the sky would turn purple at this point, the wind would whip up, and the livestock would start acting weird. I had never met these people before. I don't know why I expected them to know what they were doing. The short phone brief I had received from my boss should have given me pause. I had among my teammates a retired guy who was imagined as our elections expert, a washed-out juicer who slept late most days, and a former Army turret gunner who was hired for no apparent reason to oversee sewage and water programs and whose most significant contribution to the effort was a decent FarmVille score. Another teammate was a former Army MP now in charge of small business development in a country the *Economist* characterized as one of the hardest to start a small business in. Another two were agriculturalists for real, albeit specializing in hogs (in a Muslim country) and large-scale agribusiness, respectively, woefully out of their lanes in Iraq. As a gang they matched well with the SIGIR warning that some PRT staff were "generally able," some were "somewhat able," many were "less able," and a few were "generally unable" to carry out their missions. I learned only later that there had already been seven team leaders for this group in the last twelve months and that my personnel were a disparate mix of people with reasonable skill sets, a number with incomplete skill sets, and some who weren't any good at their jobs. The programs they had initiated reflected months of constantly changing guidance from the Embassy. The team liked to soothe over the horrors of war with whiskey and conveniently kept in the filing cabinet a bottle of some horrific Missouri rotgut. The team members' expectations, I came to know, were variously for blind support, for unconditional appreciation, or for me to pretty much leave them alone. To me, these were by and large people aggressively devoted to mediocrity, often achieving it.

But all that perspective would come later. Next up was a meeting to discuss the purchase of pregnant sheep for a small number of local widows. For $25,000 we'd buy the widows pregnant lambs to raise. They'd then sell the offspring. It seemed like a good enough idea, helping widows, so I asked the team how they had determined the cost of a pregnant ewe. My colleagues had asked one local sheik for a price. I asked why they hadn't sought several prices to compare; they said that would have been inconvenient. They implored me to sign off on the idea "to make things easier." Like the extra cash for McBlazer, this was "normal."

I asked how many lambs a ewe could be expected to produce in a year (the correct verb is "to lamb," as in "The ewe is ready to lamb now"), what the going price was for a lamb, and what a decent income was for a widow in Iraq. No one knew the answers. How would the widows be selected? The sheik selling us the animals would select the recipients from his extended family. He would also teach the widows sheep raising but would take from them the first healthy lamb in return. How would the widows get by if they would not be able to keep the firstborn lamb? Not our problem. We needed only to sit back and tell the Embassy how well the project was going. The team claimed they had never been held accountable for money spent. They explained that previous leaders would sign everything without question, like a high school substitute teacher.

I wouldn't sign, and it looked like things were at a stalemate. As I wondered how to get out of the room and maybe grab a taxi to, say, Paris, Ms. Sharon, our Iraqi American adviser, broke the silence by announcing I did not trust her. I'd never met her before and ten minutes into the relationship was too early to not trust her, or trust her. She began crying and ran out of the room. I asked Mel if he had drafted the project and, if so, why he did not seek multiple prices and resolve some of the issues. He said Ms. Sharon had done the work. Did Ms. Sharon have an agricultural background? Mel mumbled no, her only previous work experience was doing office work in Chicago.

My first real workday in Iraq was done. I flew back to FOB Hammer and went to bed fully expecting to be killed in my sleep by McBlazer. Unfortunately, I was not.

Tribes

A FOB was a village, populated by tribes who rarely intermingled except on business and who had little in common except for the fact that they were all at this same place at this same time in Iraq.

Soldiers

The largest tribe on any FOB were the soldiers. This was their war, and in a way they were the reason most every other tribe had migrated to Iraq. At first brush it was easy to sort the soldiers into clichés—redneck gun nuts, high school dropouts, tired Southern guys, the barracks intellectual, the kid from Brooklyn—every one of them a type for the next *Saving Private Ryan*. They dressed and walked alike and shaved their heads, allowing you to stop thinking at the first stereotype if you wanted to. The Army was a big place, and once you identified a type chances were there were more of him or her around. But after you were living on the FOB for a while you got to hear their stories. Ran away from an evil girlfriend, needed money for college, father said get a job or get out, that sort of thing. Each of them was proud to serve but each of them had at least another reason that they carried around for joining the military, their own little secret weight. Few Rambos at this level.

The soldier tribe distinguished itself with names and mascots that spoke to the odd feedback loop between Iraq war reality and American pop culture. Many units had names like Mighty Warriors or Spartans, with logos all clearly based on the movie *300*. Others liked death-inspired names such as Death Dealers, Gravediggers, Ghostriders, and the like, with logos ripped from the Eddie character on Iron Maiden album covers. A few old-timers clung to Indian names like Crazy Horse Platoon or Gunslingers, usually with flaming-skull logos that used to feature on biker jackets. The names were not creative and, when applied to nonmartial subunits like the finance office or the medical team, seemed out of place.

KBR White

KBR (Kellogg Brown and Root) conducted the backstage portion of this war. They hired people in the United States to come to Iraq and run the generators, fix the plumbing, and do all the maintenance and logistics stuff because there were nowhere near enough soldiers around to do those things. After the soldier tribe, these people were the largest group on the FOB. Not all contractors worked for KBR, as many were subcontractors and sub-subcontractors (over three hundred US companies had people in Iraq), but everyone referred to tribe

members who were contractors simply as KBR. At the peak
there were an estimated 150,000 contractors of various types in
Iraq. They were almost uniformly white, male, and from the
southern United States (or maybe they all just talked that way).
Some who had been in the military, however briefly and incon-
sequentially, spoke of their former service constantly. This
impressed the soldiers in exactly the same way a dropout who
continued to hang around the school parking lot impressed
high school juniors. These guys often referred to other men as
"brother" and liked to dress in "tactical" clothing, made by the
5.11 company. You could tell 5.11 clothing by the vast number
of unnecessary pockets all over the shirts and pants. I had a pair
of such pants myself, with over a dozen pockets, each with
Velcro and snaps and D rings and all sorts of accessories. If you
filled all the pockets, you wouldn't be able to climb stairs. The
KBR men imagined themselves as Chuck-Norris-the-young-
martial-arts-killer but instead mimicked Chuck-Norris-the-
aging-caricature. The six-figure salaries KBR paid them were
augmented with free trips home and all sorts of benefits. These
costs were of course passed on to the taxpayer and may have been
part of the reason soldiers were paid only mediocre wages—even
in the military there was only so much money to go around.

KBR Brown

What the KBR White personnel did not do was anything dirty,
dark, or dangerous, such as cleaning latrines, digging holes,
unloading things, guarding places, or serving food. Exclusively
young male workers imported from Sri Lanka, Indonesia, India,
and other Third World garden spots did those jobs. KBR paid
them low wages by American standards but pretty good wages

by Sri Lankan standards, which undoubtedly made those jobs more palatable. There were rumors of virtual slavery, always unconfirmed, of workers tricked by middlemen into becoming indentured for their travel costs and finishing their year in Iraq in a downward spiral of debt. KBR Brown people were mysterious. Almost none of them spoke more than a handful of English phrases ("closed now cleaning time, you wait, no use toilet broken") and I never encountered them except behind the serving counter or cleaning things.

The servant assigned to the bank of latrines behind our office was there from morning until late at night. He had a small folding campstool that he sat on, sliding it leftward over the course of the day to keep within the shadow of the latrine bank as the sun moved. Seemingly from the near-constant scrubbing, his right arm was muscled while his left was thin. He was so thorough that our latrines were closed for cleaning a good part of the working day. He smiled at everyone but said nothing. I do not know where he used the latrine himself or if he was subjected to some sort of Dickensian regime where he had to use substandard facilities whilst laboring in ours. One day he was gone, replaced by a younger man who spoke so little English that we never knew if the replacement was a punishment or a promotion for our old guy. It all gave the place a last-days-of-the-Raj feel, when it did not give it a we-are-slave-owners feel.

KBR Green

The members of KBR Green were also white but they carried weapons and did security things on the FOB. Most were Americans, with a few exotic Brits and shady South Africans thrown in. Many used to work for Blackwater, which escaped account-

ability for its alleged evil actions by cleverly changing its name
to Xe. Not to their face, most people would call these guys
mercs, not contractors, in that they carried weapons on behalf
of the US government, sometimes shot at Iraqis, but were not
soldiers. This is what the military would look like without its
senior NCOs—a frat house with guns. This tribe differentiated
itself from the soldiers. They especially favored fingerless leather
gloves—think biker gang or Insane Clown Posse fanboys. Popular was a clean-shaven head, no mustache, but a spiky goatee
about four inches long teased straight out. You know the look
from late-night convenience-store beer runs.

They walked around like Yosemite Sam, with their arms out
as if their very biceps prevented them from standing straight.
They were bullies, of course, flirting inappropriately with the
women and posturing around the men. Count on them to wear
the most expensive Oakley sunglasses and the most unnecessary gear (gold man bracelets, tactical hair gel), a bit like *Jersey
Shore* rejects.

The tribe worked out in the gym a lot, as did the soldiers.
The KBR Green guys, however, ended up huge, ripped, and
strong while the soldiers just ended up strong, leading to
whispered discussions about large-scale steroid use. Aggressive tattoos on all exposed skin seemed a condition of membership, especially wavy inked patterns around the biceps and on
the neck. They all let on that they were former SEALs, Green
Berets, SAS men, Legion of Doom members, but they could
not talk about it. Nor did they disclose their last names (soldiers, however, *only* had last names, as in "Tell Smith to get on
that"). Instead they tended to go by nicknames like Bulldog,
Spider, Red Bull, Wolverine, Smitty, or Sully. Extra credit if
you caught one using a nickname left over from *Top Gun*. If

arrogance was contagious they'd all be sneezing. All Aryan, all dudely.

Other Contractors

This might have been the most distant, opaque, and self-enclosed tribe of all. There was a group of young Filipino men and women who ran the concessions on the FOB. No one knew how they got there or how they supported themselves with something like an embroidery shop on a military base. They did not engage in conversation for any reason, though all spoke English, perhaps because the women were hit on by the soldiers and contractors approximately ten million thousand times a day. The American military had always depended on a community of Filipinos to staff its bars and curio shops, so these workers may have been brought in just for tradition's sake.

In addition to the Filipinos, there was a contingent of very young men from the slums of Uganda who guarded most US military facilities. Paying Ugandans saved money because guard duty was boring until it became suddenly violent; then it was boring again for a long time. Americans did not want to do such work, and it cost a lot of money to get Americans to volunteer for the Army. Ugandans were cheap, they knew about weapons as former child soldiers, and for some reason the contracting company had a connection into Uganda. (The Embassy used a different contractor and so was guarded exclusively by Peruvians.) For the same reasons Mexicans cut your lawn at home and Hondurans cleaned your hotel rooms, your Army guards came from Uganda.

The Ugandans were a sad group. Manning the guard towers at night, they could sometimes be heard singing to one another, sweetly calling out to a fellow countryman two hundred meters downrange but even farther away from home than we were. The Ugandans spoke only a few words of English and just could not deal with the cold. In winter, the desert gets cold at night, and for months Iraq is semitemperate and often rainy. Guarding things tends to involve standing still or walking around outside, a bad mix for the Ugandans. As soon as the weather cooled off even a bit, they would break out an amazing collection of nonstandard colorful wool caps and heavy gear, to the point where one poor guard was wearing hockey gloves to keep warm.

I'd learned from one of the US citizen supervisors that a Ugandan guard might make $600 a month, with much of it owed back to the brokers and middlemen who helped him get from Africa to Mesopotamia. The Ugandan could also be fined by his supervisor up to $100 for lying, sleeping on duty, or some other infraction. A US citizen supervisor might make $20,000 a month, tax free, with benefits, while in Iraq.

Iraqis

Aside from the few local Iraqis who ran the small hajji shops and commuted in and out of the FOB, there were two other groups of Iraqis who worked with us, the Iraqi Army and our own imported Iraqi Americans.

The US Army units I embedded with sometimes trained the Iraqi Army, who were now our allies against the insurgents. The Iraqi Army did not live on the FOB but often hung around for meals and to buy things at the franchise shops. The training seemed a bit nonsensical at times, consisting of either rote simple drills or over-the-top complex vehicle maintenance lessons that were a struggle for the many nonliterate enlisted

Iraqis. Training the Iraqis was clearly regarded by our side as among the worst duty in-country. The Iraqis were gleefully a Third World organization, in the opinion of the soldiers who worked with them, and were considered sloppy about discipline, casual with their weapons, and adamantly untrainable. As a token of our conquering them, the Iraqi name tags were in English and Arabic, which must have pissed them off every time they looked in the mirror. An Iraqi general who often visited always had his ten-year-old son with him, wearing an exact replica of Dad's uniform, right down to the gun in a holster. An American soldier who tried talking to the kid discovered that the gun was real—and loaded.

The Iraqi Americans were another tribe who worked primarily as translators. They had immigrated to the United States and become citizens years ago. Most were from Detroit or Chicago, recruited by subcontractors for their alleged language skills. Most of our Iraqi American translators were employees of an Alaskan Native–owned business. This business had one employee in the States, an Alaskan Native far away in Alaska, and subcontracted to some other business that recruited Iraqi Americans in Detroit and sent them to us in Baghdad. To help support minority businesses such as those owned by Alaskan Natives, the US government offered them an advantage in the otherwise competitive bidding process, a sort of contracting affirmative action, even as they subbed out 100 percent of the work. It seemed like a get-rich-quick Internet scam, but it was legal.

Like KBR White personnel, the Iraqi Americans had six-figure salaries, free trips home, and sweet benefits. Many of them had not lived in Iraq for years yet we used them as cultural advisers. Some had lived entirely within Iraqi American communities in the States and spoke poor English but served as translators nevertheless. Some were Kurdish and/or Christian, which no doubt impressed the Muslim Arabs we primarily interacted with. The supposed best of the bunch served as BBAs (bilingual and bicultural advisers), each with a specialty topic such as "agriculture" or "women's issues." Many were nice folks but knew nothing about agriculture or women's issues. One BBA who worked with us was named a "women's program adviser" by sole virtue of her having lady parts; when we moved to another FOB, she became an agricultural adviser because we needed an ag adviser and she was there. No one will ever know how much of our failure in reconstructing Iraq was caused simply by bad translation and subject-matter ignorance, but it would be a decent percentage.

Money and Our Meth Habit

We lacked a lot of things in Iraq: flush toilets, fresh vegetables, the comfort of family members nearby, and of course adult supervision, strategic guidance, and common sense. Like Guns N' Roses' budget for meth after a new hit, the one thing we did not lack was money. There was money everywhere. A soldier recalled unloading pallets of new US hundred-dollar bills, millions of dollars flushing out of the belly of a C-130 cargo aircraft to be picked up off the runway by forklifts (operated by soldiers who would make less in their lifetimes than what was on their skids at that moment). You couldn't walk around a corner without stumbling over bales of money; the place was lousy with it. In my twenty-three years working for the State Department, we never had enough money. We were always being told to "do more with less," as if slogans were cash. Now there was literally more money than we could spend. It was weird. We'd be watching the news from home about foreclosures, and I'd be reading e-mails from my sister about school cutbacks, while signing off on tens of thousands of dollars for stuff in Iraq. At one point we were tasked to give out micro-grants, $5,000 in actual cash handed to an Iraqi to "open a busi-ness," no strings attached. If he took the money and in front of us spent it on dope and pinball, it was no matter. We wondered among ourselves whether we shouldn't be running a PRT in Detroit or New Orleans instead of Baghdad.

In addition to the $63 billion Congress had handed us for Iraq's reconstruction, we also had some $91 billion of captured Iraqi funds (that were mostly misplaced by the Coalition Pro-visional Authority), plus another $18 billion donated by coun-tries such as Japan and South Korea. In 2009, we had another $387 million for aid to internal refugees that paid for many reconstruction-like projects. If that was not enough, over a bil-lion additional US dollars were spent on operating costs for the Provincial Reconstruction Teams. By comparison, the recon-struction of Germany and Japan cost, in 2010 dollars, only $32 billion and $17 billion, respectively.[7]

While a lot of the money was spent in big bites at high levels through the Embassy, or possibly just thrown into the river when no one could find a match to set it on fire, at the local level money was spent via two programs: CERP and QRF. CERP was Army money, the Commander's Emergency Response Pro-gram. Though originally provided to address emergency human-itarian needs and short-term counterinsurgency costs, this nearly unlimited pool of cash came to be spent on reconstruction. The local US Army Commander could himself approve projects up to $200,000, with almost no technical or policy oversight. Accounting was fast and loose; a 2009 audit, for example, found the Army could not account for $8.7 billion in funds.[8] It might have been stolen or just lost; no one will ever know. The Army shared its money with us at the ePRTs, partly out of generosity, partly out of pity, and partly because individual military units were graded on how much cash they spent—more money spent meant more reconstruction kudos on evaluation reports.

The PRTs lobbied State for their own funding source for their own projects, separate from the mother Embassy's adventures and independent of the Army. State's original idea was that the PRTs would use Army money in the field while the Embassy pursued its own course. Success depended on how well we could convince the military to use its money for our goals. Of course only when goals overlapped would that plan work. Often it did not work and the effectiveness of the early PRTs was limited.

In summer 2007, State gave in and created the Quick Response Fund (QRF). QRF was the Surge's signature civilian resource. It was PRT-directed development money, independent of the massive financial resources of the military. The problems began almost immediately, when the Embassy's Regional Security Office sought to extend its control to vetting all PRT assistance to Iraqis. But Iraqis, wary of who would have access to their personal information, would not consent to a complex security review. PRTs thus lost much of their initiative, missing opportunities during early lulls in violence. A change was necessary, vetting was loosened in line with practicality, things picked up, and as of late September 2008 QRF had approved 2,065 programs and disbursed almost 50 percent of its funds. Between 2007 and 2010, QRF spent over $152 million. That relatively small sum doesn't tell the whole story. Army CERP outfunded State QRF roughly ten to one throughout the war, with many of the projects directed by or turned over to the ePRTs. Overall, billions were spent.

Despite the common wisdom that spending money was easy, our work was encumbered by two unconnected problems: the ever-changing mandate on what to do and the cumbersome procedures that accompanied QRF.

The Embassy, isolated in the Green Zone, was obsessive in insisting on its ability to shape events in Iraq through our project work. It tasked the PRTs with broad goals, or LOEs (rhymes with Lou, Lines of Effort), such as "building a civil society," as if we were playing a freakishly long version of *The Sims*. The ePRT then had to make up local projects to show efforts were being made in each Line of Effort. Sometimes it was simple, as with an agriculture LOE: we would pay for pesticide spraying on date trees like Saddam used to do. With vaguer themes such as "empowering women," the LOE was a harder target to hit and we flopped around with conferences and small-business funding. Added to the LOE issue was the constantly changing guidance on scope, where the rules seemed more compulsive than obsessive. One fiscal quarter the emphasis from the Embassy would be on limited, immediate-impact projects, while three months later we'd be told to shift to long-term efforts. We would abandon our date spraying to focus on a derelict water plant, until a blast from above would flip us back to smaller stuff like buying school supplies. Somewhere in Foggy Bottom this all came together in the form of bar charts and PowerPoint widgets and made sense to people far removed from the dust and grit.

Every one of these project ideas had to be funded, and because they were local initiatives that usually meant Embassy approval for QRF money. Most QRF-funded projects entailed

three stages of review. After the ePRT completed a multipage
grant application and a multipage summary, the proposal was
entered into a database to be reviewed by a committee at the
Embassy. From there, proposals went to Washington, where a
separate committee reevaluated them. The review committee's
questions illustrated the blind-leading-the-blind style of management. Instead of asking why an ePRT wanted to spend
$22,000 to produce a stage play in Iraq, the committee asked
why the play's director needed five production assistants. Project budgets in dollars might get sent back for the ePRT to do
the simple conversion into Iraqi dinars, adding weeks to the
processing time. Rarely was a project rejected for lack of merit.
The ePRTs quickly learned to focus on form, knowing little
would be said about substance. The review process substituted
petty corrections for any semblance of broader policy guidance.
Such guidance came in the form of nested series of reports,
murky documents we combed through for clues. Here's one:

> QRF proposals must be tied to the recently updated PRT
> Work Plans, per OPA and QRF policy. Proposal themes
> in the database are based off the old PRT Maturity
> Models and will continue to be used as broad indicators
> of targeted impact. The QRF Team will coordinate with
> the OPA Plans Office to ensure proposals fall in line
> with PRT strategic objectives.

New regulations in late 2009 required 50 percent Iraqi
participation in any project that benefited the government of
Iraq, when paid for by State (the military had no such restrictions somehow). The change came after our own Government
Accountability Office (GAO) noted that the government of Iraq

had posted a $52 billion budget surplus between 2004 and
2009.[9] The new policy was implemented to create local buy-in
and also to lessen the burden on the American taxpayer. The
State Department determined this 50 percent cost share could
be "in kind." The Iraqis wouldn't need to come up with actual
cash for their half but instead could contribute goods or services. It would be like, when your HMO asks for a co-pay, your
offering to wash dishes in the cafeteria instead. A better anal-
ogy would be your telling the HMO your time is worth $40 an
hour and your co-pay is already covered by time spent in the
waiting room.

Since the Iraqis had no intention of paying for the things we
wanted to do, the State Department grew increasingly creative
in deciding what constituted an in-kind contribution. This was
not out of a desire to help Iraq; waiting for the locals to pony up
cash or supplies made it difficult to complete projects neatly
within one's twelve-month tour of service, a real bar to getting
pats on the head from one's boss. For example, my ePRT proposed spending $22,705 to purchase a set of legal reference
books for the Mahmudiyah courthouse.[10] The Iraqis needed to
come up with about $11,000. Since getting the courthouse to
hand over actual cash proved impossible, we accepted in-kind
payment as follows:

> The Government of Iraq will provide an equipped library
> room with electricity, bookshelves, furniture, a computer,
> a heating and cooling system and an expert librarian. The
> life expectancy of the books is at least ten years. Although
> the amount contributed in housing, utilities, etc. for the
> books is difficult to quantify, an average salary for a librar-
> ian is $400 a month. The salary for a year is $4,800 and

> thus the salary for ten years without a pay increase is
> $48,000. At a minimum, the GOI is contributing $48,000
> to this project.

By quickly calculating the books would last ten years, adding
in the value of an existing unused room actually built by
Saddam, and multiplying the fictional salary of a librarian who
never would exist, we discovered that the Iraqi "contribution"
was $48,000, or roughly four times what we had asked them
for. But of course the only money spent was American. It was
almost as if we ended up owing them money.

In another case, we identified the need to train the water
plant operators of the Ministry of Municipalities and Public
Works.[11] Textbooks were expensive, and the cost was over
$38,000, including $50 a week per student for lunch (we could
never get people to show up without a giveaway of some kind).
That meant the Iraqis owed us $19,000 for their co-pay. Instead
of cash, the ministry agreed to continue to pay its employees
their full salaries while they attended our training. Cost to the
US, $38,000; cost to Iraq, salaries they were going to pay any-
way. This satisfied the cost-share requirement. Plus we bought
lunch. The Office of the Special Inspector General for Iraq
Reconstruction (SIGIR), in a report to Congress entitled *Hard
Lessons: The Iraq Reconstruction Experience*, showed that it at least
retained a sense of humor about our spending, quoting Dick-
ens's *Great Expectations*: "We spent as much money as we could,
and got as little for it as people could make up their minds to
give us."

There were other absurdities. We were not allowed to order
things through the Internet. When we needed something not
available in Iraq, such as veterinary supplies, we had to pay an

intermediary to order it through the Internet, for which he charged a 30 percent fee. QRF also did not allow shipping via diplomatic pouch or the military postal system, so our 30 percent vendor tagged on a 100 percent markup for shipping and local customs costs, including bribes. The QRF rules thus increased the price of Internet-bought goods by 130 percent. Iraqi businesses sprung up just to make a profit ordering things for us off the Web. A meth habit might have been cheaper.

Then there were the work-arounds. During the month of Ramadan devout Muslims fast during the day, with an Iftar, a big meal, after dark. People often turned this into a social affair, and businesses hosted Iftars for their clients. It seemed like a decent idea that we at the ePRT might host an Iftar or two. Here's the guidance on using QRF money for such a purpose:

> Regulations prohibit the use of QRF funds for entertainment and religious purposes. An Iftar would be considered both an entertainment and a religious event and not an allowable QRF project.

Iftar expenses would be allowed, however, if QRF funds were incidental to a programmatic activity (wink, wink, nudge, nudge). For example, if a speaker gave a lecture during the Iftar event, the meal expenses would be allowed. With a little thinking outside the box, QRF could fund an Iftar.

QRF rules contained other such work-arounds. For example, we could not give more than $3,000 to a company or contractor. We could, however, give an unlimited amount to an NGO. If I wanted to rebuild a school, I couldn't hire a contractor. If a contractor registered himself as an NGO, say

"Mr. Contractor's NGO," I could give him as much money as he could swallow. A tsunami of corruption overtook the previously sleepy NGO registration office, run by the government of Iraq—you had to pay to play and registration was not cheap.

Transparency International, in its 2010 ranking of the world's most corrupt countries, gave Iraq the number four slot (beaten only by Somalia, Myanmar, and Afghanistan). Pre-2003-invasion Iraq was ranked only twentieth worldwide in corruption, so it was obvious all of our money had contributed something to the country.[12]

Caring about Trash

Heat in Iraq was like opening the door of the oven to peek at a pizza, *whoosh*, right in your face, making you close your eyes against it. Breathe in too fast and it rolled all the way down like a hot drag off a joint. The light was bright, bleaching color from most things. Stepping outside, you couldn't see anything for a moment as your eyes struggled to adjust. The high one day was 111 in the shade, only there was no shade. The next day it spiked to 125. It was the heat, oh Christ, yes. In the shower, the water from the cold tap was almost too hot to stand under. You wished there were batteries that could soak it up now and parcel it out in cold places later. Sliding from air-conditioned building to air-conditioned building was much like our stay in the country, boarding our armored vehicles on one base and getting out at another, passing through Iraq long enough to feel the heat but not long enough to have to do more than tolerate it. They lived with the stench of piled-up garbage and fetid water.

We lived with our AC. Outside was Iraq, hot and sharp; inside it was cool and dark.

In our air-conditioned isolation, it took years to realize we needed to think about things like garbage and potable water. What had happened all around Iraq since the chaos of 2003 was a process of devolution, where populated areas lost their ability to sustain the facilities that had constituted civilization since the Romans—water, sewage, trash removal—things that made it possible for large numbers of people to live in close proximity to one another. Shock and awe had disrupted the networked infrastructure that allowed cities to function. What had been slow degradation through neglect under Saddam became irreversible decline by force under the United States.

The collapse of civil society left a void that the bad guys had rushed to fill. Stories circulated of neighborhood militiamen commandeering shuttered power plants and private generators for the public's use, turning the militants into local heroes. In some poor areas, especially in the south, Iranian charities were a primary source of propane, food, and other services that people expected the government to provide, as Saddam had more or less done. It had finally dawned on us that providing reliable basic utilities was critical to a successful counterinsurgency. The PRTs were put on the case after earlier efforts by megacontractors like Bechtel and then the Army Corps of Engineers had failed.

Almost daily my team and I would go out into the field. We'd strap on body armor and helmets and load into armored vehicles for the soldiers to drive us out of the FOB. We rode in either armored Humvees or large monster trucks called MRAPs, mine-resistant, ambush-protected carriers. These sat high off the ground and were covered in antennas and crazy electronics designed to thwart the battery-powered triggers that set off IEDs and mines along our route. The best thing about the MRAPs was that they were hermetically sealed against nonexistent chemical weapons and thus possessed near-nuclear-powered air-conditioning. You could crank that stuff and form frost. The MRAPs were so high off the ground that the turret often tore down the spaghetti web of pirated electric lines strung over most streets, lessening our popularity every time we drove in. Our parade of four or five vehicles, armed with nasty-looking machine guns and tough-looking soldiers, would nonetheless roll through small towns and slums to arrive at whatever dilapidated building served as the center of US-appointed local government. (By common consent no one was allowed to comment on the paradox of creating a democracy by appointing local leaders. It just wasn't done.) As we drove, trash was a fact anywhere we looked, like the sun and the dust. The MRAPs specifically equipped to look for roadside bombs even had giant blowers welded to their front bumpers to whip garbage aside and expose the IEDs. For a poor country, everybody seemed to have a lot of things to throw away. Even though the trash was rarely collected, there were huge dumps filled with acres of it. You couldn't help but be reminded that for all the counterinsurgency ideals about living among the people, we still lived near Iraq but not in it; on the FOB you couldn't drop a Snickers wrapper without two people telling you to pick that shit up.

My team and I met with Yasmine, the local municipal services director, to ask about the status of trash collection in the area. The central market posed the most difficult challenge because of the volume of daily trash, the limited equipment to haul it away, and security. Concrete T-wall barriers located on either end of the market served as security checkpoints, making access for collection vehicles difficult and thus unpredictable. Without daily removal, there was both a danger to public health and increased risk, because garbage was a prime location for hidden explosives. The accumulated trash everywhere also signaled the utter lack of concern by the US-supported Iraqi government for the welfare of the people it ruled since the departure of the evil dictator who, officially, was better off gone. Freedom for sure, but unfortunately it was the freedom to not care.

Yasmine described the lack of experience among officials and corruption as further impediments. What the country needed, she said, "was educated, honest technocrats." She mentioned officials who underspecified and then overpriced equipment so they could skim money. She lamented the lack of budget preparation. Without local input, the Baghdad-based Ministry of Municipalities developed the budgets for all the regional areas. This was especially galling for a long-term resident like Yasmine, who sincerely cared about the place she had grown up in. While she noted the frequency (and unproductiveness) of her meetings with US-appointed politicians, it disappointed her that fellow municipal directors never even bothered to show up for the coordination sessions she tried to schedule. This was all in spite of a multiyear, $250 million contract let out by the United States to hold good-government classes for these same Iraqi officials to teach them to be better bureaucrats. The contract was held by the US Agency for International Development (USAID), which, while a part of the US government, did not report to the State Department. So, although I knew from talking to Yasmine that such a program was running in my area, I had no way to influence it or learn more about it except if Yasmine told me things or I happened to find some information on the Web, management by Google. The USAID representative would not tell me what he was working on. He would report to his boss, who would write a summary for my boss, who often remembered to forward it to me. We did not play well together.

Like USAID and State, the Army and State also had a hard time getting their vision for what we were doing in Iraq synchronized. The Army can be hard to understand. They often did things their own way for their own reasons, a bad idea when you were talking about the coordinated conduct of foreign policy and reconstruction of Iraq in support of our national security goals. While the State Department saw its mission as trending toward bigger picture stuff, the Army often focused on more immediate things. The argument was not a simple one—was it right to focus on a five-year water plant rebuilding project while local children suffered from dysentery that could be relieved by bringing in truckloads of bottled water daily? In an ideal world one could do both, satisfy the short-term need while working in the background on the long-term solution. We, however, worked in rural Iraq one year at a time, not an ideal world, and so couldn't agree on what was best to do.

Everyone did agree garbage was a problem, and it was obvious the solution was for someone to pick it up. But trash pickup was the archetypal example of everything that wasn't working with reconstruction. "If the trash isn't picked up soon," said the Brigade Commander, "somebody will plant an IED in it and one of my boys will die. I'm going to pay people to pick up the trash now rather than wait for the Iraqi government." It was a pragmatic approach to security but one that provided a disincentive for municipalities to discharge their responsibilities. As long as the United States would pay for trash pickup, why should the municipality? Using Coalition cash rather than Iraqi institutions set back efforts to foster self-reliance. Many small towns gave up lobbying the central government for money, knowing the Americans would pay for everything. Instead of encouraging growth and capacity of civic functions, our massive hemorrhaging of cash discouraged them. When we grew weary of paying or were diverted by some other shiny object, there was no one around to pick up the problem, and the trash piled up.

Complicating matters further, the contractors we employed often distorted local labor markets. The USAID inspector general found wages paid for trash pickup by its Community Stabilization Program were higher than the average for even skilled laborers. It was more lucrative to be overpaid by the United States to pick up trash than it was to run a shop or fix cars. Possibly people went out and found more trash to throw around so that they could be paid by us to pick it up. We overpaid for everything, creating and then fueling a vast market for corruption. It wasn't so much that we were conned, it was as if we demanded to be cheated and would not take no for an answer.

When Secretary of State Colin Powell warned President George W. Bush that after invading Iraq he would assume responsibility for thirty million people, it is doubtful anyone thought that years later the US government would be worrying about trash pickup in the central market of a rural town outside Baghdad. The maps consulted in dark, air-conditioned bunkers with blue arrows indicating an armored thrust had no strategy to offer for getting the garbage picked up. Had anyone known that nearby Baghdad produced eight thousand tons of trash a day, most of it now left uncollected just like in Yasmine's town, would we still have invaded? It was unlikely that anyone in the United States knew trash collection was now a major front in the Global War on Terror. To be honest, who cared about garbage in Iraq, except maybe the Iraqis who lived around the central market? They, after all, stayed in our war while we only visited.

There was no AC in Yasmine's office. One window had only busted-out glass, there was no electricity most of the time, and any AC unit would be stolen within the day. Near the end of our visit, Yasmine looked out the broken window at the garbage being picked over by goats in the heat and let out a sigh. Though Iraqis will shout their opinions at you in the street and wave their hands like a crack-crazed aerobics teacher to make a point, it was hard to sort out what they said from what they meant from what they thought you wanted to hear. Add in a bad translator who reduced three minutes of rapid speech to "He disagrees but loves all Americans and Obama president" and you often had no idea what was going on.

Yasmine spoke carefully, making sure the translator got it right. She was of an age, she said, where all she could remember were the wars with Iran in the 1980s, the long years of sanctions in the 1990s, and the US occupation from 2003. She asked when her daughter would lead a peaceful life. I thought she was talking to me, so I told her I didn't know and it was time for us to leave, as our security team said we had been in one place too long. Good-byes in these situations were always hasty and awkward, as the traditional final greetings and handshakes were hard to negotiate when everyone was pulling on their helmets and body armor, with the scratch of Velcro cutting through the exchange of formalities. Wearing that gear outside made a hot day even hotter, so it was nice to get back to the air-conditioning. Nothing was resolved with the trash pickup, but in the AC it seemed far away, for us at least, though maybe less so for Yasmine. She's still out there, we're still in here.

Water and Sewage

In a desert country like Iraq, nothing mattered more than water and its evil twin, sewage. Water was what allowed humans to live in the desert, and providing water and sewage facilities on a large scale had been the responsibility of the rulers of Mesopotamia since nearly prehistoric times. The United States eventually came to understand that providing such services was also part of our own responsibility and that configuring the nascent Iraqi government to take on these tasks was key to our counterinsurgency strategy.

With water on the brain, we once again mounted our armored convoy and drove off the FOB and into Iraq proper. The ride out to the vast nonworking sewage treatment plant took us through the usual postapocalyptic landscape, with ditches on each side of the road filled with greenish muck (neither water nor mud, and why was it green?).

The plant was built in 1963, and it had not been improved

on since then. It processed no sewage; shit literally flowed right through it. Raw goop, possibly related to the green muck we saw in the ditches, poured untreated into the ancient Tigris. Back in 2004, when the war was still trendy and the Coalition of the Willing was still in play, the Belgians and the Japanese promised to rebuild the sewage plant and even committed a bunch of money. Belgian and Japanese engineering firms drew up plans, produced blueprints, and created a giant three-ring binder of bad English to describe what was to be done. A big problem in Iraq with water, sewage, and power delivery was measuring capacity (for example, how much water you had) and use (how much water you used). Under Saddam and continuing to this day, water and power were free (not socialism when we endorse it), so most facilities had no measuring devices. The capacity of the new plant was set to account for the projected population growth in Baghdad in the future, originally defined as 2027, later revised to 2005 to cut costs. It was far too expensive to have that much future. Then, the plant's future was put on hold altogether. The Belgians got out early, the Japanese engineers never visited the plant, and all sectarian hell broke loose.

Our sewage plant wasn't the only one that needed tending, as a large and growing proportion of Iraqis had no access to potable water. The early occupation authorities initially seemed to recognize the problem, and a $680 million cost-plus water reconstruction contract granted to Bechtel called for the water supply to be repaired within one year. The United States also selected Bechtel as the prime contractor for the bulk of the $4.6 billion in sewage projects funded by the occupation.[13] Only nothing was ever done.

Early notice that reconstruction was not reviving Iraqi

infrastructure came in December 2004 in a report issued by the Post-Conflict Reconstruction Project of the Center for Strategic and International Studies. The report enumerated the ways the impact of US efforts in Iraq had been stunted. Only 27 percent of funding committed was actually spent on reconstruction per se. The rest was siphoned off, with 30 percent spent on security, 12 percent on insurance and international salaries, 10 percent on overhead, and 6 percent on profits. An additional 15 percent was lost to a standing line item in Iraq work—fraud, corruption, and mismanagement.[14] The year 2004 was bad in general for water and sewage in Iraq. In a typical head-spinning strategy shift, the focus moved to security and oil production as State took over from the Coalition Provisional Authority. Work on water, sewage, and electricity was considered "too slow to have an immediate impact," and so spending on those areas was deliberately cut by half.[15]

By late 2005, the number of people served by sewers had dropped from a prewar 6.2 million to 4.5 million. Water treatment capacity dropped in the same period from 3 million cubic meters per day to 1.1 million cubic meters. When Iraqis were asked in an August 2005 poll how often they had safe, clean water, 72 percent responded "never."[16] In the neighborhood where I worked, tests in 2010 showed the local piped water was full of E. coli, heavy metals, and sulfuric acid. Though the locals dared not drink such water, they used it for bathing, causing skin diseases and other health problems. The nonoperating treatment plant we were visiting was to be part of the solution.

The plant was in the custody of a single engineer. As I learned over the course of several visits, he was trained in Moscow through a friendship pact arranged under Saddam. He was quite a character, the Engineer, spinning stories about drinking vodka in Bulgaria and picking up Russian women with the lure of then-valuable Iraqi dinars to be exchanged on the black market for rubles. A thin man with glasses he could never keep from sliding down his nose, the Engineer liked to think out loud with a pencil and paper. His office was very big but very empty. Over the last few years his staff had dwindled from seventy-five to twenty-eight, with many of them killed and others simply vanishing, maybe to live in Jordan, maybe to move in with relatives, maybe left for dead in the green muck. He told us of calling the office to say he'd be in at ten and then not showing up until three in the afternoon or of leaving a note in his appointment book saying he was away on vacation and instead sneaking in to work at night, all as a way of staying alive amidst the anarchy unleashed by our invasion.

The Engineer confirmed that the plant processed no sewage, though he and his twenty-eight workers remained on the payroll. He showed us the Korean Daewoo TV and Dell laptop a US Army unit had given him. He watched the TV all day but was not sure what to do with the laptop, so it was unplugged and dusty. He had left the filmy plastic in place on everything, even the TV screen. It made the devices look sad.

Although no redevelopment had been done, the Belgian and Japanese money was still sitting in an account somewhere. However, the Belgian and Japanese governments were not interested in visiting the sewage plant. The Belgians had no embassy in Iraq and seemed a little surprised the project was still on the table. The Japanese rarely left their tidy enclave in the Green Zone and certainly were not coming out to a sewage plant no one remembered promising to pay for in 2004. The Belgian and Japanese engineering companies, on the other hand, were still interested in making money, though neither cared to send any staff to Iraq and instead were soliciting bids from local Iraqis to do the work. The Engineer was confident they would do a good job, because most of the Iraqi companies bidding were fronts for Turkish construction firms, who would bring in Arabic-speaking engineers from Jordan. Proud of this Coalition of the Willing, the Engineer noted that few Iraqis would have an important role on the project. We Americans would help by being the eyes and ears on the ground for the Belgian and Japanese governments, at least until we closed down our ePRT in line with the military drawdown. Bids would arrive in a few months, followed by a three-week evaluation period. (Many of the companies bidding were fronts for the same company in Turkey and would file dummy bids against themselves. The Engineer would try to figure out which bids came from the same company and would then use that information to get the lowest price.) As per the 2004 agreement, the companies would leave behind all of the trucks and heavy construction equipment imported to do the work. The Engineer planned to sell these items to raise money for maintenance. His problems were far from unique. A Government Accountability Office report in 2006 had listed the challenges the United States faced in rebuilding and stabilizing Iraq: security, lack of direction, and problems with basic maintenance, and, related, lack of Iraqi buy-in.[17]

Security costs were affected by the significant increases in attacks against Iraqi and US forces after 2003. The State Department reported security represented 16 to 22 percent of the overall costs of major infrastructure projects. But the Engineer already knew about the high cost of security. He told us two of his biggest needs at the sewage plant were guard towers and machine guns. He laid out a quick history of all the valuable things stolen from his plant over the years. He whipped out a plastic folder in which he had a hand-drawn plan to build guard towers around the plant, set so that at least two machine guns covered each meter of the perimeter. The Belgian and Japanese engineering companies had not spec'd for machine-gun towers, such things not being part of sewer plants in Belgium and Japan. The money provided would not cover the cost of the towers. This was an issue in which the Engineer hoped God would intervene.

The old saying "Any road will get you there if you don't know where you're going" seemed to apply. Our efforts, well meaning but almost always somewhat ignorant, lacked a broader strategy, a way to connect local work with national goals. Some days it felt like the plan was to turn dozens of entities loose with millions of dollars and hope something fell together (monkeys typing might produce Shakespeare). Inadequate performance data and measures made it difficult to determine the overall progress and impact of US reconstruction efforts. You don't know what you don't measure, leaving much of our work to have all the impact of a cheap direct-to-DVD martial arts movie.

For this sewage plant, the Engineer and we had essentially no goals or metrics other than wishing things would improve. The lack of metrics—other than hope—was a common feature in our reporting on water, sewage, and other essential services, leaving us without an agreed picture of what success would look like. The absence of metrics was handy, however, in that it always allowed for the possibility that things might improve around the next temporal corner. For example, from an ePRT report:

The Team visited a sewage treatment facility where the installation of concrete pilings has delayed progress for months. We met with the contractor and the Baghdad Sewage Authority's (BSA) resident engineer. Both men were optimistic about the facility and felt progress was being made. This is due in large measure to the hiring of a new consultant by the BSA. The current cooperation between the BSA, project contractor and the new consultant was refreshing and suggests they have the ability and willingness to solve difficult problems.

It turned out that they had neither the ability nor the willingness. Nothing happened.

The Government Accountability Office also found that the reconstruction program was hampered by Iraq's difficulty sustaining new and renovated infrastructure projects. "Sustainment reviews" conducted in 2007 suggested projects transferred to Iraqi control were not being adequately maintained. For example, two Baghdad power stations rebuilt with US funds were not operational, largely owing to insufficiently maintained equipment.[18] The Iraqis, quickly realizing that "free" facilities came with long maintenance tails, started refusing to accept projects. SIGIR noted that the Iraqi government had not accepted any transfers since mid-2006, and even in 2008 "only limited progress had been made in establishing an asset transfer process."[19] By 2010, the Iraqi government had taken on only three hundred of the fifteen hundred reconstruction projects we tried to hand over. The rest have been "put on the shelf," because they were too shoddy to continue, didn't meet any existing need, or were incomplete and lacked the documentation, plans, and contracts that the Iraqis would require to finish them.[20]

The Engineer was again in agreement. Even if everything was fixed and operational some future morning, the sewage plant got only two or three hours of grid electricity a day, well within its needs in 1963 but short of the demands of 2010. Discussions with the Ministry of Electricity were under way, the Engineer promised, and he was optimistic that under a new, not-yet-elected government the ministry might give him the necessary juice. Just at that moment the power failed, and it was dark and quiet in the Engineer's office. The Daewoo TV stopped screaming an Egyptian soap opera. The Engineer said not to worry, because a generator separate from the plant ("a good one, from China, not the older Russian one") powered the office and would soon kick in. He passed around a wooden box that smelled of tobacco but was filled with candies. We all had a caramel until the diesel stench overpowering the sewage stink signaled the generator was working.

Apart from the electrical issue, the Engineer had another problem that would prevent him from processing the poop of the future: lack of skilled staff. He needed 228 people to run his 1963 plant, had 75 in 2003, and after the sectarian deaths was now making do with only 28. Of course, the plant was not currently operative, thus reducing his personnel needs. The new Belgian and Japanese equipment would require trained people, and the Engineer had no budget to hire anyone. One of the Army's idiosyncratic rules prevented CERP money, the deepest pocket, from being used for training. Again, the Engineer was hoping God would intervene. It was probably his best strategy.

Even with local Iraqi buy-in, the obstacles seemed insurmountable. At the ground level, local officials found it no easier than we did to navigate the complex and corrupt bureaucracy above them. For example, in Narawhan, northeast of Baghdad, they had a lot of water. It was "raw water," green and dirty, but it was indeed water and could be cleaned up and made drinkable through the aged treatment plant squatting in the midst of a large Sunni settlement. There were a lot of thirsty people there, as the few water lines in the community had been illegally tapped to the point where at a certain location downstream the water pressure was too weak to push liquid through the pipe. It seemed like a sweet deal—there was plenty of raw water, a start on a pipe system, and an existing treatment facility. At the cost of several million dollars, we proposed to the local officials that we would build pipes to haul in more raw water, rehab the treatment plant, and tidy up the existing system.

All that was needed was to get the Iraqi Ministry of Electricity to run power about two hundred meters into the treatment plant. Simple as this sounded, it was the single point of failure for the whole project. Nobody took charge, everybody kept asking the United States to fix the line, and delay followed delay. This one thing could have brought potable water to many people, but in the absence of a responsive bureaucracy nothing was ever done. We ran out of time and went home. The people do not have water.

This failure was not limited to one site. When I arrived in Iraq, the Al Qudus water treatment facility had not been working for two weeks because of a defective controller board for the generator. There was no dedicated electric power at the site. The operator explained that the pumps for the compact units were undersized and often broke down. In addition, the chlorine system for the two units was broken. He blamed contractor shortcuts during construction for the plant's abysmal performance. No one knew where to start. The people do not have water.

Clearly, large-scale water and sewage work required technical expertise and project management skills far beyond what local officials or our small ePRT could handle. Recognizing that big ventures took years while our evaluation and promotion cycles took months, a Major hoping to make Colonel noticed a thing called Mobile Max while trolling the Internet. Mobile Max was a trailer-mounted, solar-powered reverse-osmosis water filtration machine. Drop one hose into any water source, add in some sunshine, and clean water would come out the other end. This would solve Iraq's water problems.

Without any checking or testing, the Army spent $3 million to buy twenty-five Mobile Maxes and ship them to Iraq, just as if they were ordering slacks off LLBean.com. Shipping the units all the way to Iraq was no small task, involving massive behind-the-scenes full-contact customs work (bribes). The equipment took so long to arrive that the Army unit that ordered it had departed Iraq, and the gear was received with much enthusiasm by the replacement brigade. The twenty-five Mobile Maxes even looked confident, bright blue with sci-fi solar panels. A test well was dug and out poured . . . not much. It seems, for its many charms, that Mobile Max could not deal well with the high-salinity groundwater found commonly in Iraq. More freshwater was needed to back-flush the salt out of Max than Max produced, meaning the rig used more water than it made. Resolution seemed to be at hand, as the Army ordered $500,000 worth of salt-filter upgrade kits, which, months later, arrived. We parked five Mobile Max units out in Iraq for testing.

The first unit choked on the salty water. The locals used it as a source of electricity, pulling some current from the solar panels until they broke.

The second unit was stolen from its public location and reinstalled at a sheik's home. Mobile Max managed the low-volume water use there just fine, and the sheik was happy.

The third unit, because of the salt in the water, needed continual maintenance and filter cleaning, which we had not provided for. Local thugs took possession and started charging people for the water in return for their protection and hiring their relatives to clean the filters. Eventually that unit broke down and the people blamed the United States for sending them shoddy equipment.

The other two units just disappeared, much like water spilled onto the desert floor. The remaining twenty Mobile Max units sat on the FOB. No one knew what to do with them, and everyone wished they would just go away. General Ray Odierno himself, noticing them on an inspection, ordered the Maxes delivered to someone in Iraq, anyone, to get them off our books. No one was ever held responsible for wasting $3 million.

When in doubt, change policy. In 2006, the Embassy in Baghdad proclaimed it was moving from the previous model of building and turning over projects to Iraqi management toward a "build-train-turnover" system. To no effect. Next, the US government declared 2008 to be the "year of services" in Iraq, but it wasn't. Neither was 2009. There was a brief policy called "Iraqis stand up while we stand down," which neither did. We finally gave up in 2010, determining water and sewage were for the Iraqi government to resolve on its own, washing our hands in full view of problems we could not solve.

The International Committee of the Red Cross in 2009 estimated that more than 40 percent of Iraqis still did not have access to clean water.[21] Back at our sewer plant, I said good-bye to the Engineer and promised to visit again if there was any news. The Engineer, smiling, was still optimistic that foreign help would intervene. He planned to learn a few words of English, and maybe Japanese, to be prepared.

Democracy in Iraq:
A Story of Local Politics

Since God first created sand, Iraq has been organized politically and socially by tribe. Essentially a series of semiautonomous, interlocking extended families, a tribe could potentially encompass many thousands of people spread across the country. In the words of a common Iraqi threat, "We will seek revenge and my tribe is not small." A head sheik led each tribe, with subtribes run by lesser sheiks, typically blood relatives. The sheiks prided themselves on long claims to power. One of the biggest big shots I knew proudly displayed in his home an elaborate family tree tracing his lineage through the Prophet directly back to the biblical Adam.

Rather than fight such a long-standing system, Saddam coopted the tribal organizations that undergirded Iraq, manipulating the local sheiks toward his own ends by giving power to some, money to others, and depriving those who crossed him of both. This system worked so well that after the United States liberated Iraq, instead of holding local elections as the starting point for converting the country into a democracy, we appointed sheiks as local leaders, with the promise of elections to follow, someday. Meet the new boss, same as the old boss.

Having appointed the sheiks, the United States then set about rebuilding a democratic Iraq, using the sheiks as conduits to push reconstruction money into local communities. The goal was to hide the US role and make it seem like all the projects were local efforts, something we made ourselves believe while no one else did. Corruption was a problem. Since the sheiks suggested projects on behalf of their communities, coincidentally they tended to benefit personally from those projects, manipulating the local people toward their own ends by giving power to some, money to others, and taking both from those who crossed them. The sheiks controlled the territory like Mafia dons, owning the big-scale projects, picking them apart, and selling off trucks and generators for profit. We tolerated this. Every gesture we made toward the sheiks was justified as a short-term but necessary expediency and every gesture toward the sheiks undermined the broader concept of real elected government.

The sheiks all wore many hats, filling the power vacuum post-2003 and exploiting sectarian differences as we fumbled around trying to create Greater Georgebushistan (peace be upon him). The sheiks were easy to deal with as they wanted our money, understood authority and violence, and could in the short term get things done. Most sheiks had a fan spread of business cards to offer you, depending on circumstances—sheik leader, general contractor, procurement guy, generic businessman, whatever you needed.

When money became scarce for local initiatives (the periodic swing in Embassy emphasis between big projects and grass-roots efforts seemed to take place every few months), the sheiks would begin to fight among themselves. In the Rasheed area, a crummy scrap of land outside Baghdad controlled by thugs even during Saddam's time, district council chair Sheik Aman was removed from his position under threat of death by Sheik Yasser, who then replaced him. During a TV broadcast Sheik Aman waived a court decision he claimed returned him to the chair and at the next meeting, displaying a flair for the dramatic and an interest in physical persuasion, he grabbed the council's official seals and stormed out. Sheik Yasser promptly held a news conference to denounce Sheik Aman for stealing the council seals. If there were limits to corruption, both men were still trying to find them. The position of district council chair was important because the United States, after creating these bodies, also used them to distribute money. Boring Iraqi district offices morphed into smoke-filled back rooms. "My favorite description is the bar scene in *Star Wars*," one ePRT member recalled, invoking a description to be repeated by every subsequent ePRT member. "Our district council chair was the Tony Soprano for the area. At meetings, he'd say 'You will use my contractor or your work will not get done.' It was all about money."

In time-honored custom, the two sheiks sought reconciliation by turning to a powerful middleman to mediate, local Iraqi Army General Ali, who commanded an entire tank division and so qualified to host the meeting. A successful reconciliation allowed both sides to not have to seek revenge to restore honor, as tribal custom would have required. Reconciliation proved successful enough that these two men shook hands and embraced. The General suggested making Sheik Aman a kind of council member emeritus, preserving his pension while upholding Sheik Yasser's position as the new chair. It seemed like a happy ending.

However, Sheik Aman showed up at the very next meeting acting as chair, claiming that under democracy he had the support of the people (i.e., a bigger tribe). After a distant relative of Sheik Yasser's was killed accidentally when a magnetic sticky bomb accidentally affixed to the underside of his personal car went off, Sheik Yasser realized the need for an extended visit with family members resident in Jordan. Democracy is messy, said Don Rumsfeld. My next trip to the council chambers revealed new pictures of Sheik Aman everywhere on the walls posing with previous US military units, as well as with General Ali and his full tank division. Members of Sheik Aman's tribe searched everyone entering the chambers. Sheik Aman assured us the precaution was entirely for our security.

The meeting began with reports about electricity, water, and trash removal. The lack of electricity impeded water delivery because pumps were not pumping. Fuel to power generators that supplied electricity to the water treatment facilities remained scarce. Whether or not fuel was siphoned off prior to delivery or after delivery, the lack of electricity crippled essential services. Irrigation canals that used to deliver water to treatment facilities now provided only intermittent service. Farms went without water because pumps lacked the several hours of uninterrupted electricity needed to enable them to push water the distance necessary. Funding for trash collection had been delayed several months and the garbage was piling up. Sheik Aman asked for comments. One of the council members started to speak but was cut off by the sheik, who stated that comments were being solicited from the public and not from members. There were no comments from the public because the public was neither aware of nor invited to the meeting.

Other council members spoke to us about the lack of any investigation by security forces after a bomb blast knocked out the street wall of the council building earlier that week, not that anyone was blaming Sheik Aman, who had been curiously called away just before the blast. What the living council members and Sheik Aman could agree on was a general sense of unease. US financial support was fading for the smaller, local projects they fed upon. Government of Iraq funding for necessary capital improvements was nonexistent, and even funding for critical essential services was unreliable. Adding to this was the sheiks' worry over their precarious position as unelected local officials appointed by the US forces—all a hearty recipe for desperation. The council might attempt to seize US government–funded project assets just to create income, we were told, nothing personal. The council worried that US disengagement coupled with the absence of central Iraqi government initiative would cause an already boiling pot to spill over. On that we could agree, and hands were shaken and kisses kissed to end another successful reconciliation. Everyone hoped to be around for the next one.

Milking the US Government

Counterinsurgency theory said that it was desperation and poverty that drove people into the arms of al Qaeda. Young men, faced with no economic prospects, no way to marry and raise a family, would be easy to recruit as suicide bombers. What else did they have to live for, the theory went. Leaving aside the possibility that some people became insurgents not because they lacked fast-food jobs and iPads but because they hated the presence of a foreign invader in their country, the Army and the State Department forged ahead with ideas for job creation. I, for example, inherited an Army effort to build a distribution network ("value chain," in propaganda-speak) for milk in our area. The previous Army unit had dropped a couple of million dollars into the project, taken some pictures, and then rotated back to the States, heroes, no doubt. The current Army unit had little taste for dairy, and so the whole project fell by default onto the ePRT and me.

We were going to change the way farmers sold milk. From year zero, Iraqi farmers in our area had raised a cow or two each. The farmers kept some of the milk for themselves, selling the excess to their neighbors. Lacking refrigeration, transportation, and an organized distribution system, each area instead sought a delicate balance between the number of cows, the number of people, and the need for milk. It worked well enough for everyone but us. Without checking with the farmers, we decided to modernize the whole milk chain to create jobs. Farmers would sell their milk to our newly built centralized collection centers equipped with refrigerated tanks, and the centers would then sell the bulk milk to dairy-processing plants, also built by us. The processing plants were expected to sell to the farmers' neighbors, who would surely be waiting around wondering what happened to the friendly farmer who used to bring fresh milk around daily.

Once the Army determined the war needed milk collection centers, they went around looking at locations, like a couple with a new baby house hunting. Putting the equipment into an existing building would obviously be quicker and easier than raising a new structure. The Army was told of a building that had supposedly been a Saddam-era dairy plant and went out to take a look. The neighborhood guy who met them explained they did not want the place. He said the plant had been a chemical weapons factory. No one had cleaned inside or removed anything, so maybe it was better the troops didn't knock around, stir up the dust, and check inside the closets. The good news, the man said, was that nothing deadly had been manufactured at the plant since 1998. The Army wisely decided to build the milk collection center elsewhere.

As I took over the project, the collection center in

Mahmudiyah was 90 percent complete and a ribbon-cutting ceremony was scheduled in a week. The center had been 90 percent complete for months, with the ribbon-cutting ceremony calendared several times. A 5,000-liter tank stood ready to hold milk collected from local farmers. But when we asked our Iraqi partner Sheik Sal about his plans for the business, such as the number of employees he'd hire, the price he'd pay farmers for their milk, and how the milk would be transported to the processing plant, he was unable to answer any of the questions.

The second Army-funded milk collection center, near Yusufiyah, was also ready to open. Our partner there, Sheik Naj, was also unable to answer any questions about operating the business, except for the one about the number of employees he intended to hire: zero. Neither man had the capital to purchase trucks for hauling the milk, to buy supplies, or to pay for the milk purchased from the farmers. This was troubling. That the Army had addressed none of these issues prior to committing millions to these centers was doubly troubling. It was relatively quick and easy to build a collection center, but slow and difficult to talk farmers into changing their way of selling milk (input) or to line up buyers for the finished product (output). Starting to think about the input and output that bookended our projects only after we had spent millions of dollars on the easy parts was like crying over spilled milk. Capital was the big issue, as without money to buy the farmers' milk at a higher price than the farmers could get directly from their neighbors, no centralized collection center could succeed. Our reconstruction planning had not considered this, so we had centers that would likely remain dry until the sheiks sold them off piece by piece after we had gone.

Still committed to the project, we visited our two milk collection centers every six weeks to see if any progress had occurred, perhaps spontaneously. On one visit, the Yusufiyah plant was padlocked shut. The kids hanging around said the owner wasn't there. (Kids were always hanging around everywhere; few attended school in rural areas, and those who did went only half days because boys and girls were not allowed to go to class together as they had been under the mostly secular Saddam regime. The new Islamic Iraq we midwifed in 2003 couldn't afford to double the number of schools, so it was girls in the mornings and boys in the afternoons.) The kids told us they hadn't seen the owner in weeks.

The second center was still not operating, but it was open and I was able to look inside the place for the first time. A few weeks earlier, after the contractor notified us that the work was done, we had sent out one of our inspectors, in this case a bilingual bicultural adviser (BBA), an Iraqi American who supposedly had a degree in engineering. I say "supposedly" because I later learned that in the rush to staff up for the Surge, the State Department had hired him and others like him sight unseen, having engaged a third-party company to conduct brief phone interviews with the candidates. No credentials were checked, which perhaps accounted for the vast numbers of not bilingual Iraqi Americans claiming to have PhDs (they were paid more for advanced degrees and so said they had them). Our BBA had signed off on this project as complete and in good order.

I do not have a PhD in engineering and so noticed immediately that there was a hole in one of the milk tanks large enough to fit my index finger. The milk-weighing station (milk is sold by weight, not liquid volume, to account for the butterfat) was rusty, another bad sign since the $500,000 we spent on this center was to have included stainless steel. The owner had not even put up the English "Milk Collection Center" placard we bought him, with an eye toward a nice photo op. When I confronted the sheik on the overall state of the facility, he simply smiled and asked for more money to build a fence.

Outside, another group of kids were entertaining themselves by throwing rocks at a three-legged stray dog. You can tell the strays' age by their missing limbs, ears, and hunks of fur, like rings on tree stumps. The dog was trying to sleep, and every time the kids got close with the rocks, the dog would get up, move a little farther away, and flop down again. The kids never moved closer and never hit the dog. The dog never moved any farther than necessary. Each side accomplished nothing but the time did pass.

We went out another time to inspect one of the milk collection centers and ended up in the living room of the sheik who'd been given the facility to run. His house, modest by any international standard, was quite nice for rural Iraq. The house was concrete, two stories, squat, with the kind of thick walls you put up if you didn't have a PhD in engineering but wanted to make sure the thing lasted. As with every other building in Iraq, wind, weather, and time had beaten the stucco to a grayish tan. The floors were cool tile. The carpets were outside on the clothesline soaking up the day's sun. The building was old, and past lives clearly lingered.

The sheik casually wore his Glock in a Bond-like shoulder holster. I had read online that under long-established tradition, an Iraqi would not typically shoot you in his own home; in many years of traveling this was the first time I'd staked my life on a cultural convention from Wikipedia. An AK-47 (the law allowed every family to own one) with a full clip leaned against the wall in an adjacent room. I was weaponless but accompanied by seven heavily armed soldiers, who took up defensive positions inside, outside, and around the living room, after searching the house, of course.

The search had brought out the sheik's mother, who said she typically didn't leave the back room when male guests arrived. Since the soldiers had wandered in on her anyway and we were foreigners, she must have thought "Why not?" and sat on a chair at the edge of the room. The sheik's father, also armed, soon joined us and took a chair facing me. With the house searched and the group assembled, tea was served, scalding hot, 70 percent sugar, in tiny glasses with a metal spoon in each. I knew then that long after I left Iraq the sound of metal tinkling against glass would rip me out of wherever I found myself and return me to this country. The sound was as tied to a place as any image in my mind.

The father was animated, happy to have guests to whom he could relate the last hundred years or so of Iraqi history. From the others' reactions, I could tell that this was not the first time he had run through this overview, and I remembered my own grandfather's wandering stories around the Sunday dinner table. The father was a practiced storyteller who explained how the family had controlled the land we and our milk collection center sat on since the Ottoman Empire, having seized it from the previous owners in a bloody struggle. One nice thing the Ottomans did was to create the first codified land ownership system for the area since Hammurabi, and most property deeds today in Iraq date from Ottoman times. So thanks to them, the father said, for titling the land to his family.

He moved on to the British, who took control of Iraq from the Ottomans. His own father had not had much good to say about the British, but they had dug the large irrigation canals in the neighborhood, and so perhaps something positive came out of all that. This was interesting because the example always held out for us in the PRTs to emulate was the colonial British, who conquered the world with good administrators. Their officers were highly educated, committed, conscientious, hardworking, and conversant in the local language—regular *Flashman in the Great Game* characters. More tea was served. We skipped quickly through about forty years to Saddam. Two relatives had been killed in the Iran-Iraq war in the 1980s. The less said about Saddam, the old man muttered, the better, and we proceeded to the latest set of invaders—me, for all intents and purposes. He had good words to say (I was a guest), but he playfully added that his impression of America might be improved even more if we gave him a new generator for the house. Eyeing the weapons and fearful of having to drink more tea, I pretended to jot a note: next invasion, bring more generators.

At that point, the sheik himself started to explain how he had originally helped the "struggle" against the Americans, meaning planting roadside bombs and the like. Then, in 2007, he decided to participate in the so-called Awakening, a program through which we paid money to Sunni insurgents to stop killing us. The program worked and in many minds was the real key to the drop in violence that accompanied the Surge. The United States recharacterized the Sunni insurgents first as Orwellian "Concerned Local Citizens" and later, more poetically, as "Sons of Iraq" (SOI, *sahwa* in Arabic) and paid them monthly salaries to stand passively at checkpoints in the areas where they used to commit violence. This also worked, and the sheik pointed out that the skinny teenagers with rifles standing around roadside shacks on our way in were some of the 142 SOI fighters he still was responsible for. Our side never explored the similarity between what we were doing with the SOI and paying protection money to the Mob.

Iraq's Shiite government inherited the *sahwa* program because we got tired of funding it and because "transition" was a theme that month. The thought in Washington was that the faster we could transition our programs to the government of Iraq, the sooner we could go home. The sheik sadly reported that no one had paid his men for their forbearance since March, nor had the government provided them with full-time jobs as promised. He hoped I might pass a note to the Embassy to goose the Iraqi government into starting to pay his guys again, as they were getting solid offers from al Qaeda (nationwide, 50 percent of the SOI had not been paid in April and May 2010, while fewer than half had ever been offered government jobs).[22] Nothing personal, he assured me by way of offering a blessing on my family, but a job was a job. These issues seemed much more on his mind than the milk collection center I had come to discuss. The center might employ half a dozen men, maybe a few more to drive trucks if trucks were ever bought. With 142 fighters to look after, these few jobs created at the cost of millions of dollars seemed sadly irrelevant.

After a lot of tea and with a bit of business now wrapped up, we all stood to exchange scratchy kisses, followed by warm, lingering handshakes, before making our way outside to continue our respective days. We forgot the problems of milk collection, or at least set them aside for now, as it was obvious that we had a long way to go before declaring victory.

A Torturous Lunch

In addition to burning up money with our projects, the ePRTs were often used by the Embassy to build relationships on the ground. This was partially because most Embassy big shots were scared to meet with thugs and killers and partially because we often handed project money to those thugs and killers and thus knew them pretty well. While we usually just shared pleasantries over a meal to keep in touch, every once in a while we got more for lunch than expected. A well-known Sons of Iraq (SOI) leader told us over dessert one sticky afternoon that he had been recently released from prison. He explained that the government had wanted him off the streets in the run-up to the election, so that he would not use his political pull to get in the way of a Shia victory. The prison that held him was a secret one, he said, under the control of some shadowy part of the Iraqi security forces.[23]

The SOI leader had been tortured. Masked men bound him

at the wrists and ankles and hung him upside down. He said they did not ask him any questions or demand any information; they simply wanted to cause him pain. They whipped his testicles with a leather strap, then turned to beat the bottoms of his feet and his kidney area. They slapped and punched him. The bones in his right foot were broken with an iron rod, a rebar used to reinforce concrete. He said it was painful, but he had felt pain before. What hurt was the feeling of utter helplessness. A man like himself, he stated with an echo of pride, had never felt helpless. His strength was his ability to control things, to order men to their own deaths if necessary, to fight, to stand up to enemies. Now he could no longer sleep well at night, was less interested in life and activities, and felt little pleasure. It was possible that the SOI leader exaggerated his story, seeking our sympathy in his struggle against the government. This was likely the only reason he was bothering to tell us what happened to him. Exaggeration was not uncommon in these situations and you had to be cautious about believing everything you heard. Still, when he paused and looked across the room, you could almost see the movie running behind his eyes, replaying scenes he could not forget but did not want to remember. The man also showed us his blackened toenails, and the caved-in portion of his foot still bore a rodlike indentation with faint signs of metal grooves, like on an iron rod, the rebar used to reinforce concrete.

The 400,000 Iraq war documents published online in October 2010 included a number of US Army reports of torture and abuse by the government of Iraq against its own Sunni citizens, most of them ignored by the US Army as a consequence of Frago 242. A frago is a "fragmentary order" that summarizes a specific requirement based on a broader, earlier instruction. As published in June 2004, Frago 242 ordered Coalition troops not to investigate any breach of the laws of armed conflict, such as torture, unless it directly involved Coalition troops. Where abuse was Iraqi on Iraqi, "only an initial report will be made. . . . No further investigation will be required unless directed."[24]

The Iraqis knew of torture. FOB Loyalty, where I spent a week, had once been home to Saddam's secret police. I had walked around and seen torture cells there. Arabic graffiti covered the walls, most of it scratched directly into the stone. Metal rings were set into the floor and walls for chaining people down. The bunk was just more stone, and there was an open hole in one corner for a latrine. The story was that Saddam hired Chinese workers to build the place, then had them murdered so they would not tell anyone what was inside. Many US soldiers who passed through had their photo taken in one of the cells, sometimes lying on the bunk, but it was too creepy for me, too many shadows. Even the tough guys found reasons to avoid the place after dark. There were voices in those walls.

The other SOI men in the room chain-smoked awful cigarettes by the fistful and told us the recent murders of four Sunnis in Tarmiyah were probably tribal revenge killings stemming from the murder of a high-level SOI in the area the previous year. Three out of the four murdered were brothers and the fourth was a blood relative. Under tribal law, they explained, when compensation was not received in a timely manner, the other side had the right to kill the person who committed the murder plus three of his blood relatives.

As for national-level violence, they explained it was all the Iranians' fault, except for the parts the Americans did ("When will you close the door you opened in our country?"). Kind of hard to disagree with the last bit, but our US military colleague

along for lunch tried pretty hard. He started out declaring himself "but a simple solider" and then wound up into a long speech
about the American democratic experiment, states' rights, and
the Articles of Confederation. I had no idea what he was saying. Our translator kept right up, however, mumbling something in Arabic, though who knows what was communicated
across the space in that room. Our simple soldier hit his stride,
raising his voice in volume while he lowered it in timbre, explaining how we all were now brothers fighting a common enemy.
This was where I would have given a cornea to understand
Arabic, because of course we had invaded Iraq and even our
stalwart Iraqi translator was having a hard time figuring out
who this common enemy was. After some side conversations,
we figured out it was "the terrorists," and each was left to define
"terrorist" for himself. Considering the men in the room controlled militias and could order revenge killings, I guessed their
definition and ours were different.

After what could only be described as a multilingual awkward pause, the search for common ground began. We finally
stumbled onto something after an older SOI man discussed his
recent trip to Iran. He described his dislike of the Persians,
stretching back some three thousand years, but noted Iranian
women were, well . . . sort of hot. He did not say "hot" in so
many words, but as our hosts smiled and clicked their teeth and
made eye gestures, it was all too obvious we had basically started
talking about how attractive Iranian women were. I learned
that one reason Iraqi men traveled to Iran was to enjoy the plea-
sures of a temporary marriage. With men free to marry multiple wives and Islam's handy oral divorce policy and lack of civic
records, the prohibition against prostitution was sometimes cir-
cumvented through a quick (several hours) marriage and divorce.

Iran was known for such things, and discreet as well, so what happened in an Iranian temp marriage stayed in Iran, baby. The mood lightened.

These meetings were supposed to increase our understanding of one another, give us a chance to resolve problems, make friends, and the like. Maybe we did so on occasion. To me, however, it was more like two sides agreeing to play a game together, but we played cards while they played dominoes, diplomacy by Calvinball rules. Unnamed assassins killed two of the men present in the next six weeks, along with their sons, victims of a string of assassinations of Sons of Iraq leaders. A week later someone murdered the man who had visited Iran. The SOI leader who claimed to have been tortured was left alive, wicked, hard, and doomed.

One Too Many Mornings

The smells first: fried something from the FOB chow hall, the sticky tang of chemicals in the latrines, cigarette smoke from the always present knots of soldiers smoking. The damp odor of mud if it rained overnight (like mushrooms, like an old basement) or if a pipe broke. My least favorite smell was rotted tobacco from the butts can, a steel ammunition box half filled with brown water and hundreds of cigarette butts molded into a gelatin. The smells did not mingle, they were layered, and I experienced them sequentially. Smell, the one sense that always seemed like a joke, gave you no rest. I could close my eyes or stuff something into my ears, but with smell I could only move away or put up with it.

My roommate woke up an arm's length from me in the small trailer. I was rarely alone. Sometimes he asked how I slept, sometimes he just made morning noises. We lived close. He snored, he talked while dreaming, he sometimes paced at night, he read in bed, he took pills to sleep. He felt freer to chat at night with the lights out, like at camp. I knew he wanted to hit on the sort of hot redheaded female captain in the Ops Center who wouldn't even give up a friendly glance, tired of being everyone's go-to fantasy, and I knew he missed his wife. He talked about being afraid. I felt the same way, so we held these conversations in a kind of jailhouse shorthand. He usually ended up talking about some event that happened to him just before I got to Iraq. Everyone was entitled to tell a story and we all were careful to keep our stories distinct. Mine never overlapped in time with his so we were each free to tell the story we wanted to tell. I learned to listen, but with only half an ear at most, because the telling was usually for his benefit, not mine. Just before falling asleep we both had a few minutes with our own thoughts, the worst time of the day.

Showers were communal, and where you showered was assigned based on where you lived. Evolved primate standards allowed me to grunt hello but not make eye contact. It was partially a way of getting along, maybe a way to create the illusion of privacy, but we weren't supposed to look at one another. Still, I saw tattoos of wavy patterns or unknown Chinese characters, names of mothers or girls, shadow pictures of lost friends. The soldiers were still kids, with acne on their shoulders. Most had short hair or shaved heads, so the need for toiletries was minimal. Some kids had no hair but the whole kit anyway, bottles of Axe and tubes of lotions for softer skin, less dandruff, better scents, a little like home. Showers were short as the hot water ran out quickly. The worst thing was to come into the shower area and hear "Oh shit," which meant no more hot water. Shaving was a big deal in the military and many people lathered up their entire skulls to shave clean each morning. They went over and over the same spots with their blue plastic razors. They could never get their heads clean enough, no satisfaction, just enough to get on with the day.

We knew a lot about one another whether we liked it or not. We cared if a roommate made noise in his sleep or, the worst sin, had poor hygiene and stank. Nobody seemed to care, however, about who was and who wasn't . . . you know. The Army had some dumbasses, and they didn't like queers, blacks, or working chicks. But that was beside the point, as this was not about liking anyone. When it rained we all got wet, and when it was too hot we all sweated together, and everybody knew what we had in common was more important than what we didn't.

Breakfast was like everything else, something that used to be shared with a selected few wives, girlfriends, or boyfriends if not eaten alone, transformed here into another communal event. Most people would make the best of it, commenting about the weather. A few would annoy the majority by trying to talk about work, and some would rush to grab the corner tables that faced toward the TV, which, whether it was on or off, showing sports or a cooking show, made a little safe splash zone to eat in in silence. The food was bland, and the Army still insists chipped beef on toast is a breakfast food, but there was always coffee and you could fill up a mug, thermos, canteen, or bucket for free to take out.

After eating, one by one we slipped away. Even in cavemen times people went off alone, maybe for sanitation, maybe because it was hard-coded in our lizard brains to do this one act privately. The nearest latrines, portable toilets, were lined up in groups of five or seven. You nodded hello to people, male and female, on the way in and out. Like on an airplane, the genders shared the facilities. There was nothing to flush, no running water, no hand washing, only a swipe of gel afterwards. The imported Sri Lankans used a large truck to suck out the tank underneath and then used cleaner water to hose down the interior. If they did it wrong the toilet paper got soaked and devolved into a goopy mess. I learned to check for paper, another new skill for Iraq. Everyone missed once but few people made the mistake twice—the lizard brain at work. People were forced together in such private ways in such public places to do their own thing, rarely acknowledging one another until they were thrown back together at nightfall.

Haircuts and Prostitution

There was only one thing you had to pay for on the FOB, and everybody needed it: a haircut. Housing was free, food was free, laundry was free, but haircuts cost three bucks. As with any other capitalist venture, you had competition. There were two places on any FOB to get your haircut.

The AAFES barbershop run by the Army followed a franchise model from base to base, so every one of them was decorated with the same freakishly weird posters showing suggested haircuts, something like posters of sixties Brylcreemed masterpieces I remembered from childhood barbershops. Here, there were only two. The poster with the white guy showed a "high and tight" (hair on top, clean-shaven sides) and the poster with the black guy showed a "high and tight fade" (hair on top, shaved sides that tapered up into the hair on top). Most of us had our heads shaved clean for the heat, the fashion, and the ease of upkeep, and for that you didn't need a poster.

The AAFES barbers were all from Sri Lanka or Bangladesh, imported into Iraq by yet another unnamed subcontractor to work for cheap. They spoke little to no English, other than barber words like *short* or *shave*. A sign of a newbie soldier was his trying to have a conversation with the barber: "You see the Yankees game on AFN?" "Short, mister?" Filling up the silence in the shop were Bollywood movies blasting at near paint-peeling volume and featuring an endless parade of chubby Indian women and male actors with, ironically, elaborately styled thick black hair. I say movies, plural, mostly as an act of faith, as it was possible that the same movie played over and over again. The American customers knew no better and the endless loop of the same film would have hammered home the feeling of life in purgatory the Third World barbers no doubt knew well.

The special thing about the AAFES barbers was that they offered a sort of massage at the end of the haircut. It did not cost extra and it lasted only a moment but, if you liked, the barber would rub his hands on your head, pound his fists on your shoulders, and vigorously scrub up and down your neck with his palms. There was a barber who'd crack your neck for you, grasping your head in his skinny arms and twisting it. Once I felt vertebrae move halfway down my spine, with pain like an angry alarm clock. Some soldiers didn't like the man-touching massage part and stood up with their hands out, palms up in the universal gesture of "hell no," while most just went with it.

Competing with the Bollywood barbershop was a small Iraqi-run place, an artifact of a 2005 campaign to revive the Iraqi economy by creating lots of small businesses, starting with ones right on the bases. Episodes of spectacular food poisoning shut down most of the falafel and kebab stands, while the market for Iraqi trinkets proved to be shallow, leaving by the time I arrived in Iraq just the hajji shops and the barbers.

The Iraqi barber on Falcon, like his brothers from Sri Lanka, had a vocabulary of about six English words, all synonyms for *short*. He favored the phrase *too easy*, meaning something you requested would be easy to deliver. "Can you cut my hair short?" "Too easy." "Can you cut my hair quickly?" "Too easy." Haircuts with this guy were indeed too easy because he seemed to deliver a shorter version of whatever your hair looked like, no matter what you asked for. It took only a few minutes given this efficient system, so this was the place to go when you were in a hurry. He also gave the closest shaves, scraping away with a single-edged razor blade he pinched between two fingers. Let a guy whose language you did not speak shave around your lips and up your neck with a single-edged piece of steel and you need never again prove your courage in any way.

At FOB Hammer the Iraqi-run barbershop was endlessly rumored to be a front for prostitution. The deal was that you waited until the other customers were not listening, then asked the barber for a "special massage." Having spoken the code, you were led to a back room for paid sexytime fun. The barbershop operated out of a steel shipping container and so even the stupidest person knew there was no back room, or any room, absent the one you were sitting in. That time after time the barber would answer "no special massage here" just made the rumor more compelling, as not just anyone could order up a girl. The rumor would shift: sometimes it was only officers who could get a girl, or the girls would not service tall soldiers, or they would go only with civilians. But in fact no one could name a single person who ever got anything more than a mediocre haircut. I have no doubt that out there in the desert horny soldiers even today are convinced that sex is available for sale through that barber. You just want to believe.

Laundry

Everyone on the FOB had their laundry done for them. The process started with you taking your approved-size laundry bag to the laundry place. Signs explained that you could bring in only twenty items at a time; two socks counted as one item. You entered a large room staffed by ever-smiling Third World workers hired for these jobs. Perhaps they were happy because their job was to count laundry, not to do something hot, dirty, or dangerous.

To get your things washed, you had to get a chit from the Third World guy. The chit required your last name, first name, the last four digits of your social security number, your rank, and your unit name. But instead of writing these things your-self, you needed to tell them to the Third World guy so he could write them. When he came from a place where the language did not have a *v* or *b* sound (both came out as *w*), Van Buren was a tough one. Vocheszowski probably just threw his dirty clothing away.

After ninety minutes of respelling your name, it was time for the counting. This served two purposes: to ensure you did not violate the twenty-items rule and to allow the Third Worlder to indicate exactly what clothing was being washed. You pulled out a wad of tangled damp stuff and said "one underwear, two T-shirts" while the guy recorded it. Then for some reason you were allowed to print your own name on the bottom of the chit and sign. Somewhere back in time there must have been an investigation into a missing piece of laundry, because after signing the chit you signed a separate form certifying that what you claimed on the first form about the contents of your laundry was accurate. Each side got a carbon-copy receipt. (They still used carbon paper, perhaps the last vestige of this once common office supply tool. Some really young soldiers had never seen it before.) There could thus never, ever be a disagreement over a lost T-shirt. Nothing could have been more certain.

And then one day, just when my skull was about to explode from yet again counting out my underwear in front of a stranger, I was handed the "pearl." You'll remember the moment in *On the Road* when Kerouac sums up his purpose in traveling cross-country: somewhere when you least expect it someone will hand you the pearl, that piece of wisdom that you needed without knowing you sought it. For me, it was learning about "bulk," and a little bit about how the Army worked. There was always another way around something. After spending days of my life on laundry chits, a soldier told me you could say "bulk" and not have to count anything. You signed yet another chit waiving all rights to contest lost items of laundry, now and in perpetuity, but in return you needed only mumble "bulk" and the counting of laundry ceased. That was my happiest day in Iraq.

A Break for Dinner

Food was the real universal, the FOB's great unifier and equalizer. We had one place to eat, a cafeteria, the DFAC, or dining facility. Everybody ate the same stuff in the same place, no special deals for VIPs, officers, or FSOs, so this, like the weather, was a neutral topic for conversation. To join in, you had to follow the script: where you were previously had way better food than where you were now. The food in the Air Force was better than the food in the Army, unless you were in the Air Force, in which case the best food was in the Navy (everyone agreed the Marines had it worst). With the exception of the Embassy cafeteria—business class versus economy but it was still airplane food—the food at one FOB was pretty close to identical to the food at any other FOB. The KBR contractors who provided the vittles all bought from the same approved stock list and prepared things the same way. As in any other large-scale industrial operation, the emphasis was on food that was cheap, easy to store, and easy to prepare and that, sadly, would be familiar to most of the people. Many of the soldiers were young kids, and so grilled cheese and corn dogs were comfort food, as thoughts of Mom and TGI Friday's were closer to their hearts than thoughts of 300-plus cholesterol counts and high blood pressure. The bulk of the enlisted corps could digest Tupperware. The "healthy bar" had turkey wings instead of deep-fried chicken wings, and the steamed broccoli came drowned in bright orange cheese goop. Seasoning meant hot sauce. Every table had bottles of hot sauce, and even in the most remote outposts it was available to kill, condition, and season anything from Cheerios to mashed potatoes to bananas.

My favorite meal was Buffalo Shrimp, a dish rejected by the Long John Silver's chain as below its already low deep-fried-everything standard. Frozen hunks of batter, some even containing hints of shrimp pieces, were soaked in oil, fried, and then immersed in a viscous red sauce that burned the hell out of your tongue. The sensation was novel, a memory of actual food having an actual effect on your taste buds, and the fiery burps that followed allowed you to keep the dream alive for hours. Buffalo Shrimp usually appeared on alternate Sunday evenings. All of the food rotated on a schedule, and I worked very hard not to memorize it. Bad enough to have to eat bright yellow Chicken à la King. Worse to have to think about it in advance.

The DFAC tried to celebrate most major holidays, with special meals like steak (Wednesday's pot roast served horizontal). Best of all, twice a year, on the Army's June 14 birthday and on Super Bowl Monday (the game was live at 4:00 a.m. Monday owing to the time difference), soldiers were permitted one can of beer. This was a big, big deal. To get your can of beer, step one was to go to a room off the cafeteria, show your ID card, and have your name checked against a list of soldiers. The line was as long as the four hundred troops inhabiting the FOB. You then had to demonstrate that your weapon was safe and unloaded and place it in a holding rack. This seemed silly until you realized that most of the soldiers had not had any alcohol for months, and even this one beer was going to do some damage. An armed senior NCO with his game face on handed you your beer, which you were required to open in front of him (no hoarding allowed). You stood—no chairs inside the room—drank your beer, and left. You couldn't trade, give away, or otherwise transfer your beer, and you couldn't drink it outside the room. I waited in line over an hour the first time to find that as a nonsoldier I was not on the list and thus I got no beer. For perhaps the first time in my life I was officially the most sober person in the room. The incident underscored our situation: if the occasional mortar rounds at night, IEDs on the roads, and sniper shots did not remind you your life was not in your control, the inability to secure a can of beer as an adult drove it home. It is always the little things.

On Thanksgiving, I participated in the military tradition of officers serving the troops, standing with the Commander and dishing out boiled-to-its-death corn from a can. The Commander ladled out brown sludge gravy, also from a can. The meal was a traditional Thanksgiving, with replicas of turkey, stuffing, sweet potatoes, and all the Norman Rockwell rest. We wore paper Pilgrim hats, as did the befuddled Sri Lankans who worked beside us. No one had explained to them what was going on, and they just did what they were told, like every other night. Many frozen turkeys were flown in and cooked to within an inch of liquefaction. Nobody seemed happy, but everyone did get a lot of food, though like our reports of success, much was ladled out while little was swallowed. The experience felt nothing like home, and I think everyone was glad when it turned to Friday.

Lunch the next day reverted to business as usual, with the featured item chicken-fried steak with gravy. The steak was a piece of old, tough beef breaded and deep-fried, then covered in grayish, glutinous gravy. The alternative selection was ravioli requiring no mastication to consume; you could suck it through a straw but wouldn't want to. To save time, many soldiers just carried it to the latrine and threw it in whole to save the trouble of processing it through their intestines. Then they ate Pop-Tarts and drank Red Bulls until no one could feel their limbs. What was the difference between roasted chicken and chicken enchiladas? Usually about a week. Cafeteria recycling was obvious as we went from chicken breasts to chicken nuggets to chicken salad until someone just finished the damn chicken.

If you were at one of the more remote locations, there was a lower region of food hell. At places too small for a proper DFAC, the meals came in large foil trays, kind of a Stouffer's frozen dinner for thirty. The Army called them T rations, of course shortened to "T rats." One was labeled "main," one "starch," and one "vegetable," and inside everything was parboiled to the point that, once it was reheated, you could play three-card monte with the trays and never know the difference. Even then the gods showed no mercy because typically one meal a day was not from a tray but from a bag. This was the bottom of the food ladder, the infamous MREs, Meals Ready to Eat, also known as Meals Rejected by Everyone or, less politically correct, Meals Rejected by Ethiopians. This was field food, stuffed into freeze-dried foil pouches. Supposedly with a nod toward the growing ethnic diversity of the military, the meals included "Chinese fried rice" and "Mexican tacos" alongside "traditional meatloaf in gravy" and "hearty beef stew," but they all tasted alike, they were too salty, and the sachets were hard to tear open. There was usually a packet of instant coffee and I saw soldiers pour the crystals onto their tongues and let them dissolve in their mouths. You did get a treat inside each MRE bag, usually a slab of "pound cake" and some candy, plus a cute little bottle of hot sauce. MREs took the idea of food as a fuel to its limits, as a full bag contained some 3,000 calories, with a cold-weather version racking up more than double that. MREs do not promote healthy digestion, and many of the older soldiers complemented them with nuts or other fiber to avoid inglorious defeat at the hands of the enemy. Each MRE retained its optimism by including an amenity kit, with a tiny bit of "Paper, Toilet Type."

There was nothing more humbling than being completely sick to your stomach with only public latrines available. The unit where I lost my last shreds of dignity was a coed trailer with ten stalls and ten sinks flushing into a communal tank emptied by our Sri Lankan slave force twice daily, Gurkhas of the port-o-john. In between the flushes and heaves of my apocalypse, a soldier threw a package of Imodium over the stall door without a word being said. At various points in my life friends have shared beer, shared food, and shared a blanket, but I can't think of a dearer gesture than the one made that day.

Basketball

On evenings when I'd get tired of reading the self-congratulatory e-mails and press releases coming from the Embassy, I'd go out to watch the nightly basketball game. We had brought a backboard and regulation hoop all the way from the States, and the soldiers played as the air cooled off. The game was three-on-three. The soldiers played in a tight, disciplined way, not moving much but just enough, aikido-like, using the smallest of muscles in the slightest of ways to make the ball go where they wanted it.

The youngest of the players was not yet nineteen. He'd been eleven years old when this war started, just a little older than the kids to whom Bush read *My Pet Goat* while New York burned. WMDs, 9/11, Colin Powell at the UN, Mission Accomplished, and torture at Abu Ghraib were events in history, like the tariffs and the Stamp Act he and the others probably tuned out in school. To them, we might as well have been standing at Sharpsburg or Gettysburg. The chances were good that this time last year at least one of the players was in high school, numbing his teachers with insistent pleas of "Why do we have to learn this? When are we ever going to use it in real life?"

I doubt any of the soldiers thought much about their high school days. What mattered now was what the Army had taught them about how to fight and of course what they already knew about playing basketball. In this place, a fortresslike home in the middle of a war in Iraq, where things existed not to be beautiful, only necessary, they were the beautiful. The way they moved, the sweat on their arms, the grace in their exertion, the failing sun behind them were all beautiful, and even the most prosaic soul would not say anything different. The Iraqis spoke incessantly about seeing God's hand at work, and watching this you could almost believe it.

The sun was dropping fast, as it does in the desert. There were no floodlights to give away our location to the insurgents who some nights still lobbed mortar shells our way. That was what made this different from a million pickup games in driveways and high school parking lots and inner-city cages: the possibility of sudden death. It gave an edge to the game. Chances were good that many of the insurgents were no older than the boys on the court. Like the players, they had grown up with this war as a fact, their daily life. The Americans had always been here and the place where we were standing had never been anything but a FOB. People had inhabited this part of the world for millennia—this was Mesopotamia, the biblical Eden—yet nothing mattered but this moment.

The light had gone, but the darkness did not seem to bother the boys on the court. They had established a rhythm and they apparently knew one another well enough that the occasional bump or muttered "motherfucker" was all they needed to keep the game going. For me, though, another day had ended. This war had been going on for years now, many years plus one more day.

Humanitarian Assistance

Being embedded with the Army was more than a way to live. I worked alongside the soldiers and was expected to carry the State Department's vision of reconstruction with me. The Army excelled at a lot of things, but planning remains its strongest skill set. Nothing is done by chance, nothing that can be planned ahead of time is ever left to last-minute improvisation. Planning occurred in stages and it was only after I stumbled into this knowledge that I got the chance to get a word in edgewise.

The military planning cycle began with an order, wish, vision, hallucination, or good idea from the Colonel. Sometimes this was specific, as in "Find a way to make Route Tampa safer by interdicting the insurgents' supply routes." Other times it was general, such as "How can we get the Iraqis to rat out al Qaeda sympathizers to us?" Occasionally the ideas fell from on high, such as "Improve conditions for women in your area." The officers tasked would get together and brainstorm, produce a document for a predecision brief with the Deputy Commander, and then refine that for a decision brief for the Colonel. Targets were designated as lethal (the supply cache they'd blow up) or nonlethal (the people they'd hope to befriend). To avoid any trouble, "challenges and issues" were sorted out at the early stages so that by the time you got to the decision brief the main thrust was pretty much set in concrete.

Without this knowledge, I'd often show up alongside the Colonel for the final decision brief, ready to add my points to the discussion. Everyone would take careful notes, nod attentively, and sometimes even ask me a question or two. They'd then go on with the brief, receive the Colonel's go-ahead, and ignore everything I had said. The first time I was bewildered, the second a little pissed, and by the seventh or eighth time I finally figured out how the system worked.

Over the course of my year I was able to intercede early to make a few helpful points, deliver the Embassy's messages, and otherwise participate in the planning and decision making. As the new guy, I couldn't be too forceful in my opinions. Still, I had learned a lot through the projects that had been dumped on me when the Army moved on. I became familiar with the larger State-DOD issues played out in miniature, the clashes between easier feel-good projects and harder long-term development. In these clashes, the Colonel and I often had to agree to disagree. I remembered the abandoned promises scattered across the landscape while the Colonel forced himself to look only forward. To him, easy projects still held the allure of a quick victory and happy PR. Every Colonel wanted to make General, and you did not do that sitting on your hands listening to the State Department tell you what you should be doing.

One of the Army's favorite feel-good projects on which we

differed was a "humanitarian assistance" (HA) drive. This had very little to do with reconstruction and was always a sore point between State and the military and between me and my Colonels. Here's how it worked: The Army contracted an Iraqi vendor to assemble ten thousand bags, all made of cheap plastic and mysteriously decorated with badly rendered images of Barbie, Disney princesses, and Japanese cartoon characters, as if the bags had been left over from something else. Inside was a package of dry beans, a bottle of water, a tin of halal beef, canned vegetables, and some macaroni. The food might make one or two meals for a family of four. Soldiers would drive around looking for places to conduct a "drop," pulling up to the chosen villages and handing out HA bags to whoever showed up to take them. Everybody liked free stuff, and so a crowd usually developed. At one drop, the crowd got a bit out of hand, and the Iraqi police beat them with sticks until a US Sergeant Major waded in and broke up the melee. Sometimes the Army handed out blankets, wheelchairs, or toys bought with US government money, sometimes school supplies or other things sent by a now dwindling group of churches and schools located near US military bases in Georgia and Texas. These boxes, along with cartons of Girl Scout cookies and toiletries, used to arrive in massive quantities in the early days of the war. By 2010 they dribbled in once a week at best, usually through the chaplain's office.

The soldiers smiled at the HA drops, which were always well attended by US Army media and PR people. The events made for terrific photos—a soldier holding a kid in his arms, a soldier smiling at a hijab-clad woman. The handouts would then commence. PR would fire off hundreds of frames of the same shot, of a smiling Joe handing a Transformer toy to a beaming

Iraqi kid. If the photographers had zoomed out a bit they'd have seen the Iraqi faces grow more sullen the older the recipient. For every three-year-old smiling over a Snickers bar, there was a gray-haired mother accepting a blanket without making eye contact. You rarely saw older Iraqi men accepting giveaways. If they showed up at all, they usually stood toward the back of the crowd, smoking, their faces hard and blank.

The soldiers knew what to say around their officers and the Army media: best thing about being in Iraq, great to see these kids happy, just doing our job, glad we could help. What they said afterward, spitting Skoal into an empty Gatorade bottle, was fuck these people, we give 'em all this shit and they just fucking try to blow us up.

Resorting to gifts to seem popular was quick and easy but, like most quick solutions, really didn't help. Once you started down the path of easy answers, your methods tended to sabotage later efforts to try the harder way. In a counterinsurgency campaign, there were several ways to make friends, most of them slow and difficult, like building relationships within the local community based on trust earned and respect freely given. Each iteration of handouts caused you to lose respect from a proud group of people forced into an uneven relationship. Iraq was not the Sudan or Haiti, and while pockets of people were malnourished, overall few were starving. Even if they were, a bag with one or two meals in it was not going to make any difference. The Colonel who ordered these HA drops thought that they made him friends among the locals. He waited in vain for the groundswell of happiness set in motion to cause local people to start turning over to us info about the insurgents in their midst.

This time, the Colonel was wrong. This was not *Dances with*

Wolves; we were not going to be adopted into anybody's tribe. I remember when we tried to give away fruit tree seedlings a farmer spat on the ground and said, "You killed my son and now you are giving me a tree?" How many HA bags was a dead son worth? If a goal of the US effort was to help the government of Iraq achieve legitimacy in the eyes of its people, what sense did it make for America to hand out food bags? Violence did not taper off. No jobs were created. The rich sheiks who controlled the territory stayed rich and in control. Giving away free stuff reminded folks of Saddam's own clumsy attempts to buy love. But you just couldn't stop the Army when it was on a roll. One of the more useful things someone said to me was that sitting still is not an Army thing. The Army sees the world through the eyes of a technocrat: for every problem (the Iraqis don't like us) there was a solution (give them food bags) that involved money (an incredible $1 million in this case). The Army was like that—they got something into their heads about making friends and before you knew it you've got $1 million worth of Chinese intellectual-property-rights-violating food bags on your hands.

The Doura Art Show

Doura had become one of the most violent neighborhoods in Baghdad, which made it a good location for a $22,000 art show courtesy of the US Army. The show in 2010 was the third such event the Army had paid for in as many years. Neither the art nor the neighborhood had improved. Doura, in southern Baghdad, once was a well-to-do, mainly Christian neighborhood and home to Baghdad's art community. The area included a university and used to have many small bookshops and art galleries. It was no Left Bank, but as Iraq went it was pretty decent. Many of the artists had earned a living sculpting neofascist statues and painting cheesy murals for Saddam by day, while practicing their own, more edgy work at night. Baghdad's minority Christian community felt comfortable living among this crowd and was accepted by the Muslim majority as neighbors.

Doura erupted in sectarian violence following the 2003 invasion's near-total destruction of civil society. Shias, seeking the prime real estate in Doura, slaughtered the Sunni residents, and both sides attacked the Christians, killing many and driving the rest to seek refugee status in Syria and Jordan. The problems with Christianity post-2003 were not limited to Doura. Before the US invasion, Muslim farmers in other parts of Iraq had a relationship with their Christian neighbors. The Muslims did not eat pork. The Christians liked pork. The farmers allowed the Christians to hunt the wild pigs native to the area. The pigs, left otherwise unchecked, would destroy crops. With the Christian population dropping post-2003 the pig population grew uncontrolled.[25] "We don't even want to plant anymore because the pigs just eat it all," said a farmer. "The Christians would bring their guns and they would hunt these pigs," he continued. "Those were nice times. They used to stay at my house and we were friends." Since the rise of Islamic sentiment unleashed by the invasion, more than half of Iraq's Christians had fled the country—ironic, in that they had been residing in Mesopotamia more than five hundred years before the Muslims arrived.

In the face of such upheaval, the secular Doura art community, faced with no more paid work from Saddam and sensing a bad time, went underground. Following the initial round of Shia-Sunni violence, the Sunnis regrouped to reclaim their turf, supported by al Qaeda, newly arrived in Iraq. The cycles of revenge were their own version of performance art, replacing Doura's previous avant-garde shows. Despite the challenge of the violence, with its juicy propaganda theme of different religions once living side by side, Doura was a popular target for our hearts-and-minds campaigns. And while the few remaining artists may not have had much left to say about religious harmony, they did still know how to throw a party. The Army poured money in to sponsor art shows. The shows produced good photos and happy news stories about the rebirth of Doura. Like the rest of this war, it was a great narrative, albeit untrue.

In 2007, the US military reported, "Only a few weeks ago al Qaeda had the Iraqi populace in Doura in the grip of terror but they've been pushed out and the people have returned to worship."[26] The rebirth turned out to be stillborn, as the violence never really went away. In 2008, you could have read about Doura's next "rebirth" in the *National Review*, where the author oozed, "I realized I had never really been to this place—I just thought I had. This is the real Doura, a neighborhood and a people reborn—thanks to the bravery and sacrifice of the US Army."[27] Except darn, *that* rebirth did not take either. Only a little later, Doura became again "the most dangerous place in the world to be a Christian."[28] Undeterred, the Army decided to celebrate Doura's rebirth once more in 2010. They gave the community $5,000 to open an art supply store, another $5,000 to buy supplies from that store to distribute to local artists, and then $12,000 to put on an exhibit to show off all that US-government-paid-for art.

The Army chose a private house owned by the artist who had received the entirety of the money for the two previous art shows and who got the $12,000 for this one as well. The art business must be good, at least for this painter, because his house was sprawling, two stories, with a swimming pool. For security, a company of US soldiers spent two days stationed there, sleeping by the pool. Outside the gates, hot and overgeared Iraqi Army soldiers ringed the house, supplemented by disheveled Iraqi police sprinkled with US soldiers who unluckily had not drawn pool duty. Each art show guest went through a metal detector and was hand-wanded for weapons. Helicopters flew overhead and armored vehicles blocked off lines of sight. After that, one was free to peruse the art.

We all wandered around inside, making happy purring noises. Two giant sculpted eagles, a throwback to the Saddam School, dominated the show. One was clad in fake gold, perched upon a Babylonian-style tower. A feminist art corner featured a reclining woman with a rooster perched between her knees (a cock, get it?). There was a giant screaming face that suggested Ralph Steadman's work in *Fear and Loathing in Las Vegas*. One small bronze featured a male figure impaled by a telephone pole, likely gay iconography. Two large paintings showed an African woman with a fruit basket balanced on her head, crying out for velvet. The Army was happy. The *Stars and Stripes* reporter gushed:

The room was boiling hot due to the sheer number of people present. A canvas of variety, it was filled with people from many walks of life—sheiks, Iraqi Security Force soldiers, local businessmen and businesswomen, US soldiers, American civilians, Iraqi children. Such different ways of life, yet everyone was smiling and talking with each other like friends. What brought them all together would have been unheard of a few years ago, but because of the progress and stability in the area, an art show was able to go off without a hitch. . . . "This certainly shows the great progress that has been made in Doura," . . . said Brigadier General Kevin Mangum. . . . "This used to be a rough neighborhood, and the fact that we can do this here, it is definitely an indication that things are becoming more stable."[29]

That Doura was reborn (again) was dubious but the Army got some nice photos and the food was pretty good. The artist who received the $12,000 seemed happy. For a few hours, we all played along with the feel-good fiction as appreciative guests. The event, however, was nothing more and nothing less than smoke that blew away as quickly as we departed.

While I waited near the gate for the armored vehicle to take us back to the FOB, one of the Iraqi police officers pointed to the blond American woman in our group and said something in Arabic. Curious, the translator and I went over to chat with the cop. He apologized for what turned out to be a crude remark after the translator falsely told him the blond woman was my wife. Apology accepted. The cop then asked what was going on inside. No one had told him it was an art show, only that he was to guard the gate and refuse entry to Iraqis not invited by the United States. He was very worried about car bombs. Happy birthday, Doura.

Three Colonels

At the Embassy or at higher military headquarters, Colonels tripped over one another on the way to chow, but on a FOB there was only one. The Colonel on a FOB was the top dog and set the to-do list for the men and women under his command. He was like a mythical god, with the final word on everything, from who went out on patrol to the hours the chow hall was open to discipline matters. Getting along with your Colonel often meant the difference between an ePRT that had transport and security and one that sat around the FOB most of the time yawning. Humbleness, a rare State Department trait, seemed to be the most useful approach. FSOs who barreled in claiming their twenty years of service meant they were peers to the Colonel, with his own twenty years in the Army, failed epically. The ePRT as a State entity did not report to the Colonel and did not take orders from the Colonel, but it helped if he believed you sort of did; most of the diplomacy I practiced in Iraq took place inside the wire.

The first Colonel I worked with was a lot like the second. A muscled Southern white male ex–football player, full of sports analogies (this must have driven the al Qaeda spies listening in insane, wondering where the hell this "goal line" the Americans were always near was) and rugged man hugs, back slaps, and extra-firm handshakes for deserving man soldiers. Female soldiers also always did a great job—don't want to offend the ladies—but they were hands-off, gotta watch that stuff. The Colonels' children probably called them "sir" and they wished their wives would, too. The two Colonels were to profanity what Monet was to oils.

Both men chewed. For those who are not in the Army or who are not NASCAR drivers, "chewing" means chewing tobacco, inserting a wad of tobacco into one's mouth, absorbing the nicotine, and every few minutes spitting out the brown juice generated. The nicotine coupled with the cud chewing could help keep you awake when needed. Since even the Army frowned on spitting on the floor, one spat into a cup or, more typically, an old Gatorade bottle. Many were the jokes about someone's accidentally picking up and drinking the brown juice but no one had ever seen a real person do it.

Both Colonels thought of themselves as old-school Army, remarking at the drop of a moment's pause on their days commanding tanks, leaping from planes, or firing big, clunky violent things. They could each probably name six or seven small animals they could kill by hand, and they preferred to have little to do with what they saw as the less vital world of counterinsurgency and reconstruction. The Colonels understood the need to give counterinsurgency its due, however, and so on their bookshelves, along with the never-read Sun Tzu (who may have been talking about the PRTs when he said "tactics without strategy is the noise before defeat") and Clausewitz, were never-read volumes by this war's celebrity warrior-intellectuals, David Kilcullen and John Nagl. General Petraeus's never-read Field Manual 3-24 occupied a place of honor on their desks.

On my FOBs, the Colonels had various objectives, but the first was almost always the same: self-promotion. That was a fight we could most definitely win.

A storyboard memorialized every significant military event, and many contrived to appear significant. A storyboard was a one-slide PowerPoint presentation. What happened was that an event, real (such as an arms cache find) or manufactured (a giveaway of canned food to Iraqis so they will love America), took place. Many photos were taken at the event and a single slide with photos and some explanatory text was created and shown to visitors, superiors, media, whomever. The two Colonels loved them some storyboard and ensured that their own photos featured prominently on each display, regardless of their actual role. The lower-ranking soldiers who created the boards seemed to roll with this with a casual acceptance; maybe it was trained in basic.

Colonel Jim (first names must be brief and masculine) had an even better version of self-promotion. He arranged for every arriving guest to have his or her photo taken outside with him, Kim Jong Il–like pictures of forced handshakes. Then, while the Colonel chatted up the visitor, prints would be made, framed, and brought in. The Colonel would autograph two copies on the spot, handing one to the often incredulous recipient and directing the other be hung in the hall outside his office.

The photos themselves were a hoot, as often the great lovable bear of a man that the Colonel was would have the photo taken with his arm around the guest's shoulder. He would certainly lock in the embrace if the person was Iraqi (foreigners around the world love being hugged by large Americans). The most awkward hugs were with those who considered themselves much more important than the Colonel, such as media stars, but rarely was there someone who didn't look at least a little bewildered in the images.

Colonel Jim had walls full of such photos, the military equivalent of a Hard Rock Café. He treasured black and whites of himself with his bosses, and one can imagine some sort of weird personal validation going on as the photos were lugged around the world and hung on each new command wall. They conveyed his importance, the way insurance salesmen put up family photos to appear neighborly. The military called these "I Love Me" walls.

Both Colonel Jim and his never-met twin, Rich (not Dick), were pretty easy to get along with but hard to work with. Getting along was as simple as reading the sports scores in the *Stars and Stripes* and having something to say about whichever team won. Working together was another matter. To be fair, my predecessors had not necessarily paved the way. One insisted his former military reserve service entitled him to special handling. At another FOB, the team leader almost matched the Colonel in his need for self-promotion, at least until performance review season was over, after which his needs turned to Internet browsing. In any case, neither Colonel had much good to say about State and saw us mostly as some useless but costly thing to protect, the equivalent of Washington's dropping an expensive outdoor sculpture in the middle of the FOB and committing the Colonel to seeing it through the war unscathed. I was a fragile Henry Moore.

Colonel Jim's vision for self-promotion was expensive projects that promised to turn the war around, as if only history would record each of them as another Midway. If his civil affairs team told him the area needed something to help with milk production, a milk-processing plant bigger than a hometown high school football field was commissioned (as in electronics, where size is measured in units of cigarette packs, here the unit of measure was an American football field). As disbelieving Iraqis stood by, a million dollars fell from the sky and a processing plant appeared in some field. Or a water cleaning facility or a hot-air balloon airport. The value of the project was always measured in the future tense. It was about the jobs it *would* create, the stability it *would* promote, the good feelings it *would* generate, and, though no one said it, the freedom it would give us to walk away after the photo session and move on to the next thing. If anyone happened to wonder aloud later whatever became of these older projects, well, hey, look at this new game changer we have going just over here . . .

Colonel Rich was a more practical man who never saw the self-promotional value in large, expensive projects. They took too long, and you could spend months stalling for time with interim storyboards for the same half-assed construction site when it was completed projects that racked up points with higher headquarters. Besides, the fashion of counterinsurgency had changed, with longer hemlines and smaller, targeted projects the vogue. Through a quick assessment of the battlefield, Colonel Rich determined that the smaller projects were boring (another freaking sewer pump) and nonphotogenic. He needed a new strategy, in line with the administration's childlike craving for successes to trumpet.

What could be better than free stuff? The Colonel hit on the idea of an almost endless series of humanitarian assistance drops. When this scenario wore out, the Army might partner up with some long-suffering Iraqi police unit and have it give stuff away while the Colonel stood behind and directed the action. After every Iraqi pantry within a couple of miles of the FOB was stuffed with bags of Army goodies, the Colonel adapted to the new conditions. He struck gold by sending out Army doctors to provide medical care in the field instead of vittles. The images were amazing—young blond, blue-eyed female doctors holding tiny Iraqi babies, Army women talking to Muslim women about women things, village elders thanking Army doctors for whatever was being handed out. The war was practically won those afternoons.

But without regularly scheduled follow-up medical care, the value was quickly diminished. Had anyone bothered to read those Kilcullen and Nagl war-theory books, they would have learned that haphazard charity had nothing to do with counterinsurgency. It worked pretty well when it came to self-promotion, however, and if publicity were democracy, this place would have looked like ancient Athens.

Mark, the third Colonel I worked with, looked and sounded like Bill Cosby. His walls had a few I Love Me photos, but the main thing you noticed in his office was an Iraqi tea set that actually got used. He would do one-armed push-ups as punishment when he was late for a meeting, and he ran at the head of the pack in every FOB 10K. He seemed a lot closer to the kind of guy you would want leading your counterinsurgency struggle, if for nothing else than his sense of humor. He and I were among the few people old enough on the FOB to remember the Three Stooges, and behind very tightly closed doors Mark would do a wicked imitation of any of half a dozen Stooges routines.

The area near Salman Pak where we sometimes worked was a nasty place, with a large number of s*ahwa*, SOI. Although the United States had bought off the SOI during the Surge and paid them to guard checkpoints, transitioning these angry young men into real jobs had since floundered. Add in the fact that several Sunni-Shia "seams" ran through the area, lines of conflict where the religious communities rubbed against each other, plus the reality that any government authority took a backseat to tribal power, and you had yourself one volatile zone.

Colonel Mark was in charge of our FOB during the run-up to the March 2010 parliamentary elections, which were to be the capstone on the US effort and allow us to hit the door running. Tensions in our area were at an all-time high. One day, Colonel Mark handed out copies of Malcolm Gladwell's *The Tipping Point* to his senior staff, with orders to read it by Saturday. For a good five days, the FOB resembled an undergrad dorm the week before midterms, with some officers chewing rapidly through the book while others procrastinated and begged for summaries and notes. For the three people who haven't read the book, the main point Colonel Mark wanted his brigade to absorb was this: With each new trend, key people exist who have more clout than others. Find these people, influence them, and they'll spread the message or trend widely enough that it will become common knowledge, self-powered and self-sustaining, the tipping point of the title.

The FOB was to turn all of its resources toward identifying

those key people in the area whom we should influence, who would then in turn help sway the larger population. The goal was to contain the violence, root out the few hard-core nasties, and locate places to spend money and do stuff that would channel the locals' anger and frustration away from disrupting the elections. We embarked on a long series of late-night discussions, some formal, with PowerPoint (this was still the Army, after all), some held spontaneously in the hallways, with cold coffee. Tough captains who led night patrols were made to sit down with doughy pay clerks to sort out who was really a tribal leader and who was merely a guy who had figured out how to take our money. People who had not always played a significant role on the FOB, such as second-line translators and quiet anthropologists recruited by the Army, rose to new prominence. The Colonel was omnipresent, encouraging discussion and challenging his staff to create an ever more complex matrix of the thugs, politicians, and cutthroats who shaped events in our region.

With the matrix done, the Colonel then used his own clout (if you thought of the relationships in our area as an uneasy truce among street gangs, the US Army was still the baddest boy on the block), money, and status to start talking. The brigade sacrificed its kidneys in a long round of midnight teas with Iraqi sheiks. Promises of security and safe passage were negotiated and some old scores were allowed to be settled, all culminating in a meeting that brought most of the right people together to hear our message. Small groups held discussions about how to ensure fair elections, who would be responsible for what, and who would need to stay the hell away from whom. Lines were drawn and deals made, some less savory than others, but an understanding was reached on how we were to get along. As each Iraqi leader thought over whether to follow us, he saw we kept our side of the deals. It was not all pretty, but the relationships that were formed made for a smooth election and laid the foundation for control and stability in a Wild, Wild West area that knew neither previously.

One of the difficult parts about counterinsurgency was that it was hard to tell when you had won. You measured success more by what did not happen than what did, the silence that defined the music. Silence did not play well with self-promotion, but it sure as hell beat the sound of IEDs.

Some Chick Event

A huge line of effort for the reconstruction of Iraq had to do with the empowerment of women. The origins of this are murky. Some of us expected the Republicans to like the fact that women could not work outside the home or drive, as well as all the other features radical Islam offered to the distaff gender. In the odd way things bounced, however, freeing women from their oppression got tied into the overall idea of liberating Iraq, with the net result that women ranked high on our collective agenda. Sure, the idea helped sell the war at home but there was always this sneaking feeling that the real reason the Bush people liked it was that it pissed off Muslim men.

Our goal, the Embassy reminded us regularly, was to turn Iraq's Islamically oppressed women into entrepreneurs and have them throw off their *hijabs* for miniskirts, liberated and free. Most Iraqi women, however, seemed less interested in owning businesses and hopping around in short skirts than in somehow finding water, medicine, and education for their non-miniskirted children. No matter. As with pretty much everything we did, our vision was not to be disturbed by anything as silly as reality. We treated Iraq as a blank slate and discarded any lessons of past experience.

Reality, even when enthusiastically ignored, is a stern teacher and so our women things got off to a slow start. No one signed up for the early business training events. Unable to raise corporate executives from the dust in the brief time allotted, we focused on locating women who would, in return for our money, form NGOs and attend a nearly endless round of conferences and seminars we paid for. It was easy for them, as little was expected other than that they pose for photos. It was easy for us as well. Two hotels, one just in and the other just next to the Green Zone, offered packages so that with a single phone call (plus money) we got a big room, food, music, and microphones. These conferences were perfect venues for Embassy speakers. They could dart out of the Embassy compound in armored Suburbans, make quick speeches composed of the words *freedom-liberation-empowerment-women* randomly rearranged several times, and then rocket back to Planet Embassy before dinner. The Embassy people could claim they had ventured into the Red Zone (actually everything in Iraq but the Green Zone was Red) and buff up their performance reviews. We would reward the women who attended with additional projects (cash) for playing along.

Both the Army and the PRTs got into this game, but the Army was always a bit clumsy when it came to the ladies. Male Colonels who would probably have felt more comfortable dragging women into caves by their hair stumbled around trying to come up with what they described as "some kind of goddamn chick event" to satisfy the Line of Effort. At our FOB the Colonel rooted down through his staff until he found a woman and then assigned her the task. The female Army Major stuck with the mission committed her befuddlement to the record.

12 NOVEMBER 2009:

> I presented the non-lethal target to the Brigade Commander. A State Department man attended and provided neither guidelines nor issues with moving forward. I relayed cost figures to the Brigade Commander. He selected the highest priced option, $22,987, because he wanted to illustrate his commitment to women's issues.

20 NOVEMBER 2009:

> The State Department man complained to the Embassy in an email, "I just found out a Major has stepped over our ePRT Women's Initiatives Advisor and is attempting to coordinate directly with the Embassy Women's Issues Coordinator. This is not protocol. Evidently, there was even a scouting trip to the al-Rasheed Hotel Saturday morning and I was not invited!"

26 NOVEMBER 2009:

> At the non-lethal target decision brief, the Brigade Commander asked whom we were requesting as the keynote speaker for the Woman's Conference. I told him I would like to pursue the women's issues Ambassador, because she projects a presence as a lifelong women's advocate. He said she was a busy lady, so make sure we did this immediately. Great choice sir!

28 NOVEMBER 2009:

> The Lieutenant in my planning cell asked if she could invite an Army band. I said roger and requested a chamber band of four female soldiers to play welcoming music.

29 November 2009:

> The State Department man said, "I have now had three differ-
> ent discussions with the Major and I am not sure if she gets it."
> I think he was saying I am stupid, which I do not appreciate.

01 December 2009:

> The Brigade Commander decided to hold the conference the
> "Army Way" without the State Department's involvement.

After another two months of back and forth, the Army held
the conference at the al-Rasheed Hotel. All the males except
one master of ceremonies left the room after lunch, while some
180 women, including a female US Army Sergeant who was
sent to monitor the event and who provided these details, stayed.
The master of ceremonies serenaded the women before switch-
ing to a DJ role and blasting out Arab pop tunes. All 180
women in the room began to dance. The group formed a large
circle, and women jumped in voluntarily or were pulled in to
dance what our shocked Sergeant, who came from Wisconsin,
called a "kind of belly dance." The Sergeant said she wasn't sure
whether it was the non-Wisconsin-type dancing or that the US
Army paid for it all that was more upsetting to her, but she
asked please not to be ordered to attend any future such events.
The Iraqis have a saying that what women want is roasted ice,
so maybe there was no way to have made everyone happy. The
Colonel, however, was very happy, as he indeed got his chick
event and could cross off another item on his brigade's recon-
structing-Iraq to-do list.

Widowed Tractors,
Bees for Widows

As the ground turned muddy with the seasonal rains Mesopotamia has always depended on to fill its rivers and cisterns, we decided to give away some tractors to help ensure the annual planting and harvest went smoothly. This required Salina.

Like many a budding entrepreneur hoping to scoop up some reconstruction money, Salina had turned herself into an NGO. She came up with the idea that we would give her NGO greenhouses and tractors and she would employ widows to farm for her. The women would have jobs and Salina would acquire a sweatshop operation paid for by the US government. The key was the widows. Of the many things Iraq lacked, it did not lack widows. We had created many of them ourselves, and so the Embassy told the ePRTs to help widows. Salina and her pods of widows were also useful in that they represented our blurry vision of women in Iraq as entrepreneurs and employed. The widows themselves were a trend, something every ePRT had to find a way to work with. The previous big trend, sports diplomacy, had not been good for widows. Few played sports. The movie *Invictus*, about how apartheid was solved in South Africa by the various races playing rugby together, started the sports diplomacy meme after the film was a minor hit somewhere in 2009. For about six months in Iraq, hundreds of thousands of dollars were spent to hold soccer matches pitting Sunni teams against Shia teams. Both sides agreed informally to stop the violence long enough to pick up American money, plus neat prizes for the winners (aw, hell, you're all winners today!) like colorful jerseys and soccer balls. There were a few hilarious United States versus Iraq matches as well, as our soldiers valiantly faked enthusiasm for soccer while getting their asses kicked by teams from local schools. The troops made jokes about how "you beat us at soccer but we beat you in the war," which never seemed funny to the Iraqi side.

With the sports trend behind us, the ePRT had a firm grasp of what we wanted our woman and her widows to accomplish. On our recommendation, the US government agreed to gift Salina's new NGO $183,420 worth of farm equipment. US policy was that grants over $100,000 needed to be administered by private firms we contracted ("implementing partners"), as the government did not trust its own employees to manage the money. The private firm took the $183,420, lopped off a 38 percent administrative fee, and bought Salina's NGO six greenhouses and three tractors.

The problems began a few days later when Salina wanted to return the tractors. A local gang had told her if she did not give them the tractors they would kill her. Salina dispatched the tractors to the protection of another thug, a sheik from her own tribe, for safekeeping. It was at this point we learned Salina had never legally formed the NGO that she said she had and to which the US government, through a contractor for a 38 percent fee, had given the goods. So now it was unclear who technically owned the tractors, which were in any case in the hands of the sheik. It was also unclear how many US and Iraqi laws had been violated, but in the meantime it was the ePRT's task to recover the tractors.

Getting the tractors back involved what we called muscular diplomacy. Our implementing partner used some of its 38 percent fee money to hire a group of rough boys to repo the vehicles from the sheik. On try number one, weapons were drawn and our crew had to back off. Try number two went a little better, with no weapons, only a little pushing and shoving. Finally, on try number three, our boys got the tractors and put them into US-paid storage. We wanted to give the tractors to another NGO, but the implementing partner was not sure that was legal. We paid the rent while the partner's expensive lawyers in Washington tried to resolve the issue. We might still be paying.

After the tractor project imploded, our ag adviser wanted something simple to work on. An Iraqi organization arose in Babil that provided beekeeping in a box; just add money and the group would set up some beekeepers. Even though the scheme cost over $1,600 per setup and one could hope to earn only about $200 a year from the harvested honey, we liked these bee projects because they were easy. The organization had worked with other ePRTs and knew our system better than we did. They recommended our ag adviser configure his project as "Beekeeping for Widows." This would make Embassy approval more likely as "_____ for Widows" scored points on the economic-capacity-building Line of

Effort, the help-for-vulnerable-populations Line of Effort (widows), and the help-for-women Line of Effort (widows again, but it counted).

The organization told our adviser that he could get fifteen beekeeping sets for just under $25,000, another plus in that the Embassy could approve such microprojects without having to go through Washington. And so we proceeded to enrich fifteen widows out of the thirty million people who lived in Iraq. A few weeks and a lot of paperwork later, the Embassy approved the money (you just can't miss with widows). It was only at this point that our project touched the ground in Iraq. Prior to this, it had existed primarily within the confines of the Embassy and our imagination.

We had not seen any reason to involve the Iraqis, though we should have, because it turned out widows were not as keen to keep bees as we thought, showing roughly the same enthusiasm as they had for short skirts. Several organizations claimed to have no widows available for us, but under pressure from the Embassy to start the initiative, we finally reached Selma, the go-to person for widows, the godfather of husbandless women. She was one Iraqi woman, but she was also an NGO and had made a lot of money working with the US military and the ePRT, acting as a kind of broker between our need for widows, our money, and said widows. For a small administrative fee, her NGO would locate fifteen suitable candidates without us having to drive around and look for them. Within a few days, copies of the national ID cards of fifteen widows were e-mailed to us (Iraq has few, if any, fax machines, because there are few, if any, landline phones left working).

Happy with our lineup, we found it easy to stare past the dour faces on the ID cards and reimagine our widows happily keeping bees. When we tried to contact them, however, it turned out none of the cell numbers worked. This could have meant they did not exist and Selma was planning to take the money and buzz away, but luckily Selma contacted them for us. Bad news: the widows wanted us to pay for taxis to take them to the training, or they would refuse to keep the bees. Our project was thus again in danger of failure. We had no money allotted in the paperwork to pay for taxi rides and would have to resubmit the whole thing to the Embassy to have it added. The widows dug in their heels (said Selma; we were never able to contact them directly) and refused to accept beekeeping gear free of charge. We did not have any extra widows to give the stuff to. We felt boxed in, knowing the Embassy expected us to make things work and would not let us get out of the deal. An interesting note: To prevent the hive from flying away and relocating, the queen bee is locked in a special cage deep within the wooden box the bees live in. She cannot escape her hive. She is forced to simply stay there whether she wants to or not—not unlike us, or even the widows—and try to make things work.

Chicken Shit

Agriculture was what we really focused on in our rural area. Whether it was sheep, bees, or a milk-collection center, the goal was always to lift up the local economy and provide jobs that gave people an alternative to terrorism. The next front in our farm war would be chicken.

Very few people outside the agricultural world know that if the rooster in a flock dies the hens will continue to produce fertile eggs for up to four weeks because "sperm nests," located in the ovary ducts of hens, collect and store sperm as a survival mechanism to ensure fertile eggs even after the male is gone. I had to know this as part of my reconstruction of Iraq. Like learning that Baghdad produced eight thousand tons of trash every day, who could have imagined when we invaded Iraq that such information would be important to the Global War on Terror? If I were to meet George W., I would tell him this by way of suggesting that he did not know what he was getting the country into. I would also invite the former President along to visit a chicken-processing plant built with your tax dollars and overseen by my ePRT. We really bought into the chicken idea and spent like drunken sailors on shore leave to prove it. In this case, the price was $2.58 million for the facility.

The first indication this was all chicken shit was the smell as we arrived at the plant with a group of Embassy friends on a field trip. The odor that greeted us when we walked into what should have been the chicken killing fields of Iraq was fresh paint. There was no evidence of chicken killing as we walked past a line of refrigerated coolers. When we opened one fridge door, expecting to see chickens chilling, we found instead old buckets of paint. Our guide quickly noted that the plant had purchased twenty-five chickens that morning specifically to kill for us. This was good news, a 100 percent jump in productivity from previous days, when the plant killed no chickens at all.

The first step in Iraqi chicken killing was remarkably old. The plant had a small window, actually the single window in the whole place, that faced toward a parking lot and, way beyond that, Mecca. A sad, skinny man pulled a chicken out of a wire cage, showed it the parking lot, and then cut off its head. The man continued to grab, point, and cut twenty-five times. Soon twenty-five heads accumulated at his feet. The sharply bright red blood began to pool on the floor, floating the heads. It was enough to turn you vegan on the spot, swearing never to eat anything substantive enough to cast a shadow. The slasher did not appear to like or dislike his work. He looked bored. I kept expecting him to pull a carny sideshow grin or wave a chicken head at us, but he killed the chickens and then walked out. This appeared to be the extent of his job.

Once the executioner was done, the few other workers present started up the chicken-processing machinery, a long traveling belt with hooks to transport the chickens to and through the various processing stations, like the ultimate adventure ride. But instead of passing Cinderella's castle and Tomorrowland, the tramway stopped at the boiler, the defeatherer, and the leg saw. First, it paused in front of an employee who took a dead chicken and hung it by its feet on a hook, launching it on its journey to the next station, where it was sprayed with pressurized steam. This loosened the feathers before the belt transported the carcasses to spinning brushes, like a car wash, that knocked the feathers off. Fluff and chicken water flew everywhere. One employee stood nearby picking up the birds knocked by the brushes to the floor. The man was showered with water and had feathers stuck to his beard. The tramway then guided the chickens up and over to the foot-cutting station, which generated a lot of bone dust, making breathing in the area unpleasant. The feet continued on the tramway sans torso, ultimately to be plucked off and thrown away by another man who got out of bed knowing that was what he would do with his day. The carcass itself fell into a large stainless steel tub, where someone with a long knife gutted it, slid the entrails down a drain hole, and pushed the body over to the final station, where a worker wrapped it in plastic. The process overall sounded like something from Satan's kitchen, grinding, squeaking, and squealing in a helluva racket.

According to our press release, the key to the project was "market research which indicated Iraqis would be willing to pay a premium for fresh, halal-certified chicken, a market distinct from the cheaper imported frozen chicken found on Iraqi store shelves." The only problem was that no one actually did any market research. In 2010, most Iraqis ate frozen chicken imported from Brazil. Those crafty Brazilians at least labeled the chicken as halal, and you could buy a kilo of the stuff for about 2,200 dinars ($1.88). Because Iraq did not grow whatever chickens ate, feed had to be imported, raising the price of local chicken. A live bird in the market went for about 3,000 dinars, while chicken from our plant, where we had to pay for the feed plus the workers and who knew what else, cost over 4,000 dinars, more than the already expensive live variety and almost double the price of cheap frozen imports. With the fresh-chicken niche market satisfied by the live birds you killed yourself at home and our processed chicken too expensive, our poultry plant stayed idle; it could not afford to process any chicken. There was no unfulfilled market for the fresh halal birds we processed. Nobody seemed to have checked into this before we laid out our $2.58 million.

The US Department of Agriculture representative from Baghdad visiting the plant with us said the solution was to spend more money: $20,000 to pay a contractor to get license plates for the four Hyundai trucks outside in the parking lot facing Mecca. Our initial grant did not include licensing the vehicles we bought. The trucks, he hoped, would someday transport chicken to somewhere there might be an actual market. Another Embassy colleague repeated the line that the plant was designed to create jobs in an area of chronic unemployment, which was good news for the chicken slasher but otherwise not much help. If employment was indeed the goal, why have an automated plant with the tramway of chicken death? Instead, fifty guys doing all the work by hand seemed like a better idea. A chubby third Embassy person who came to the plant for the day, huffing and puffing in body armor, said the goal was to put more protein into the food chain, which might have been an argument for a tofu factory or a White Castle.

How many PRT staff members does it take to screw in a lightbulb? One to hire a contractor who fails to complete the job and two to write the press release in the dark. We measured the impact of our projects by their effect on us, not by their effect on the Iraqis. *Output* was the word missing from the vocabulary of developing Iraq. Everything was measured only by what we put in—dollars spent, hours committed, people engaged, bees pressed on widows, press releases written. One team leader noted, "Numbers are at times more explicative than words. Being successful in Iraq often was consequent to the number of times ePRT members could have a hands-on approach to their work. Team Leader alone has been on 170 missions since January." The poultry plant had a "business plan," but it did not mention where or how the chickens would be marketed, assuming blindly that if the plant produced chickens people would buy them—a poultry *Field of Dreams*. Without a focus on a measurable goal beyond a ribbon cutting, details such as how to sell cold-storage goods in an area without refrigeration fell through the cracks. We had failed to "form the base of a pyramid that creates the possibility of a top," the point of successful development work.[30]

The plant's business plan also talked about "an aggressive advertising campaign" using TV and radio, with the modern mechanized chicken processing, not the products per se, as the focus. This was a terrific idea in a country where most people shopped at open-air roadside markets, bargaining for the day's foodstuffs. With a per capita income of only $2,000, Iraq was hardly a place where TV ads would be the way to sell luxury chicken priced at double the competition. In a college business class, this plan would get a C– (it was nicely typed). Once someone told the professor that $2.58 million had already been spent on it, the grade might drop to a D.

I located a report on the poultry industry from June 2008 by the *Inma* Agribusiness Program, part of the United States Agency for International Development (and so named for the Arabic word for "growth"). The report's conclusion, available before we built our plant, was that several factors made investment in the Iraqi fresh-poultry industry a high-risk operation.

1. Lack of a functional cold chain in order to sell fresh chicken meat rather than live chickens;
2. Prohibitive electricity costs;
3. Lack of data on consumer demand and preference for fresh chicken;
4. Lack of competitiveness vis-à-vis frozen imports from Brazil and USA;
5. Lack of critical mass to achieve a break-even cost in slaughterhouse operations;
6. Lack of Integrated Poultry Farming to lower working capital requirements.

Working capital is a very high roadblock in poultry. Even though the growing cycle is only 7–8 weeks, farmers have to finance almost 5kg of feed for each bird. Electricity cost is probably $.12–$.15 per bird per cycle, and chicks cost $.70 each.

In the light of current circumstances Inma does not recommend the revitalization of the fresh poultry industry in Iraq as a priority until a proper cold chain is restored and affordable grid electricity available.

Despite the report's worrying conclusion that "there are no data on the size of the market for fresh chicken," the Army and the State Department went ahead and built the poultry-processing plant on the advice of Major Janice. The Major acknowledged that we could not compete on price but insisted that "we will win by offering a fresh, locally grown product . . . which our research shows has a select, ready market." Major Janice had got it wrong about having done market research suggesting a role for fresh halal chicken and had in fact ignored advice that said no data were available on such a market.

A now defunct blog set up to publicize the project dubbed it "Operation Chicken Run" and included one farmer's sincere statement, "I fought al Qaeda with bullets before you Americans were here. Now I fight them with chickens." An online commentator named Jenn of the Jungle added to the blog, proudly declaring:

> This right here is what separates America from the swill that is everyone else. We are the only ones who don't just go, fight a war, then say hasta la vista. We give fuzzy cute little baby chicks. I love my country.

So, to sum up: USAID/Inma recommended against the plant in 2008, no marketing survey was done, Major Janice claimed marketing identified a niche, a business plan was crafted around the wish, not the data, $2.58 million was spent, no chickens were being processed, and, for the record, al Qaeda was still in business. With this in mind, and the plant devoid of dead chickens, we probably want to wish Major Janice the best with her new ventures. Telemarketing? Refi sales? Nope,

Major Janice left the Army, and the US Department of Agriculture in Baghdad hired her. Her new passion was cattle insemination, and we learned from her blog, "You don't just want semen from bulls whose parents had good dairy production. You may want good feet, good back conformation or a broad chest." Just what you'd expect from a pile of bull.

Soon after my first chicken plant visit we played host to three Embassy war tourists. Unlike the minority who traveled out on real business, most people at the Embassy rarely, if ever, left the Green Zone during their one-year assignments to Iraq. They were quite content with that, happy to collect their war zone pay and hardship pay and hazardous duty pay while relaxing at the bar. Some did get curious and wanted to have a peek at this "Iraq" place they'd worked on for months, and so they ginned up an excuse to visit an ePRT.

A successful visit meant allowing them to take the pictures that showed they were out in the field but making them miserable enough that they wouldn't come back and annoy us again without a real reason. One gang of fun lovers from the Embassy who wrote about water issues in Iraq decided to come out to Indian Country. At the ePRT we needed to check on some of the wells we were paying for (i.e., to see if there was a hole in the ground where we'd paid for one; we faced a constant struggle to determine if what we paid for even existed), and so the opportunity was heaven sent. The bunch arrived fresh from the Green Zone, two women and a man. The women still wore earrings (we knew the metal got hot and caught on the headsets) and had their hair pulled back with scrunchies (anyone who had to live in the field cut it short). The guy was dressed for a safari, with more belts and zippers than Michael Jackson and enough pockets and pouches to carry supplies for a weekend. Everyone's shoes were clean. Some of the soldiers quietly called our guests gear queers.

Everywhere we stopped, we attracted a crowd of unemployed men and kids who thought we'd give them candy, so the war tourists got multiple photos of themselves in their chic getups standing next to Iraqis. They were happy. But because it was 110 degrees and the wells were located in distant dusty fields an hour away, after the first photo op or two the war tourists were quickly exhausted and filthy, meaning they were happy to not do it all again.

We took two more tourists back to the chicken plant: the Embassy's Deputy Chief of Mission (who proclaimed the visit the best day he'd ever had in Iraq, suggesting he needed to get out more often) and a journalist friend of General Odierno, who was thus entitled to VIP treatment. VIPs fly, not drive, and so tended to see even less than regular war tourists. Their visits were more highly managed so that they would stay on message in their blogs and tweets. It turns out most journalists are not as inquisitive as TV and movies would have you believe. Most are interested only in *a* story, not *the* story. Therefore, it was easy not to tell the journalist about the chicken plant problems. Instead, we had some chickens killed so the place looked busy. We had lunch at the slaughter plant—fresh roasted chicken bought at the market. The Iraqis slow roast it like the El Salvadorans do and it was juicy, with crisp skin. Served lightly salted, it simply fell apart in your mouth. We dined well and, as a bonus, consumed the evidence of our fraud.

Midcourse Correction

A thousand years ago, on day one at my ePRT, I had been out-raged by Sheep for Widows, fuming over the obvious waste of $25,000 for something so unlikely to enhance the reconstruction of Iraq. In the intervening months, I'd had a fast tour through any number of projects that achieved the same level of uselessness, albeit at frighteningly higher costs in money, effort, and time. The PRTs had been working in Iraq for three years before I arrived, but you'd sooner be able to lick the back of your own neck, as the Iraqis would say when something was impossible, than see any real results or progress. I had expected a rational system in Iraq. Instead, what I found was a Wonderland-like game where the goal seemed to be to throw a stone into the water and make no ripples. I was beginning to understand the rules: Someone at the Embassy would create a Line of Effort that fit a political need in Washington. A PRT or an Army unit would think up a corresponding project at dinner, secure funding over the weekend, and hire a contractor by Tuesday. Iraqis would watch a million dollars fall from the sky and a milk collection center would pop up. Then we'd hold a ribbon-cutting ceremony and move on. Reconstruction was a lot like the war itself, almost existential. We fought the war because we were in Iraq to fight the war. We ran projects because we had money for projects.

In spite of myself, I had overcome my initial shock and awe at the titanic wastes of money I had become responsible for managing. Things that were surprising the first time around became business as usual by the third or the fifteenth repeat. Take the Ready-Made Clothing factory. We spent money to train local women to work there, hiring sewing teachers, paying rent on a building, buying sewing machines, and acquiring some other bits and bobs. We gave the big money to the factory owner, who pocketed $200,000 to turn all this into the Mahmudiyah Women's Sewing Training Center. We justified the expense by again claiming the project would "accelerate economic development by providing much needed skilled labor." Someone reviewing the proposal wrote in the margin, "What will happen if these women are trained and the factory can't hire them?" That proved to be the key question, because as the $200,000 was spent, Chinese imports began arriving in Iraq, such that a shirt from our facility cost 10,000 dinars, while a shirt from China cost 3,000 dinars. The factory staff dwindled from a thousand to forty even as our training program ran its course. We turned unskilled, unemployed women into semiskilled, unemployed women. This outcome was better than our carpet-weaving training classes in the same neighborhood, which local gangsters co-opted, one even using children as "trainee" bonded workers until we shut them down.

Or take the Kuba beef-processing plant. There we spent $170,000 to build the plant before giving it to the man who owned the land. He did some beef processing for three months, then moved to Dubai and rented the plant to someone else. That person processed beef for three more months, then abandoned the plant entirely when his delivery truck broke down. Four extended families had moved into the abandoned plant and now lived there as squatters. Someone (it might have been us, we're checking) was still paying for a guard, whom we asked to meet. One of the squatters said the guard had a second job and so did not have time to spend at the plant. The soldiers pulling security for us gave candy to the kids who lived in our abandoned facility, all out of practiced habit.

There were also veterinary clinics, crucial to improving local agriculture, since healthier animals produced more meat and milk and bred better. At our clinic, medicinal solutions were stored in empty liter soda bottles because of a lack of clean glassware. Most medicines had run out; Saddam had ordered the last shipment under the UN Oil for Food program. Amazingly, the UN had just delivered some medicines ordered years earlier, though they had expired in 2008. The doctor said, "Under Saddam we at least got medicines once in a while. Now we are free, but we don't have medicine." Nor did they have clean water. Our conversation:

ME: How do you get water?

VET: We dig a well.

ME: How is the water?

VET: It is too salty to use, so we throw it away after pumping it.

The staff instead bought water from a vendor and carried it in bottles to work. The head vet was an older woman who had majored in English. With an eye toward some future ePRT project, I asked her what the clinic needed most and she said, "For me to leave here and live in America. Give me a scholarship."

Fed on this daily diet of absurdity, I became inured to doing little and expecting less, and it was gallows humor fun to mock art shows and make jokes about widows trying to eke out a living. I was agreeing to coast along, possessing sight but no vision.

The problem was that coasting wasn't good enough. I was going to have to fail more or at least spend more, spitting out black and white to swallow whole the overripe range of grays my position called for. The message was delivered Lima Charlie (loud and clear) when the Empire struck back, calling me into the Embassy for a come-to-Jesus session over my canceling the Sheep for Widows project. People had complained. Buccaneer sheiks were our friends. Widows were trending up. The staff whined to my boss that none of the previous team leaders had ever asked for costs and metrics. The staff reminded him that they had spent millions without a question being asked. Of course, these statements were true. Everybody did it. The State contractors did it, USAID did it, the Colonels did it. Our job was not to think in or out of the box but to retrace endlessly the outline of the box itself.

My boss laid out my many faults, speaking slowly, a common State Department habit left over from a lifetime of d e a l i n g   w i t h   f o r e i g n e r s. His boss had political ambitions, and so most of his sentences were guarded passive-aggressive barbs consisting of the words *mandate*, *robust*, *empower*, and *team building*. The two men spent an hour reviewing my performance as failing to meet their unillustrated standards, concluding that I should not bite the hand that fed us. My six team leader predecessors had found plenty of ways to spend money, after all, while the number of new projects I had initiated was lamentably low. My sector did not have a failing vocational school, as was then in vogue, our rug-making sweatshop had closed down, unemploying several indentured slave widows, and we had stopped putting money into the beef plant. The Army was keen on building a factory to make medical alcohol from dates after a hospital gases project imploded and I had failed to show enough false enthusiasm. The two bosses together were like the anti-Diogenes, shining a light into the moral darkness, looking for someone else to embrace their hallucinations of what State was to do in this place.

The words were officially correct and carefully chosen ("Leverage the power of our money to enhance the economy," "Reach out with new projects, evaluating their success instead of criticizing their potential"), but what was unspoken was clear enough: "Stop making a fuss. No one cares about the money, we have lots of money, and *not* spending it angers people. We all know we are not going to really change much in Iraq, so just do your year in the desert. Don't bring us down with you. We all have careers to consider."

My boss closed the meeting by mentioning that he would soon retire from State into a consultant job with the Army, advising on future Iraq reconstruction projects at, I imagined, about double his current salary. His boss was due back in Washington for Senate confirmation hearings that would see him appointed Ambassador to a strategically important country. Me, having been reeducated, I was dismissed back to the field to try to do better.

The Embassy Lawn,
Where the Grass
Is Always Greener

The World's Biggest Embassy (104 acres, twenty-two buildings, thousands of staff members, a $116 million vehicle inventory), physically larger than the Vatican, was a sign of our commitment, at least our commitment to excess. "Along with the Great Wall of China," said the Ambassador, "it's one of those things you can see with the naked eye from outer space."[31] The newly opened Embassy was made up of large office buildings, the main one built around a four-story atrium, with overhead lights that resembled sails. If someone had told us there was a Bath and Body Works in there, we would not have thought it odd.

The World's Biggest Embassy sat in, or perhaps defined, the Green Zone. Called the Emerald City by some, the Green Zone represented the World's Largest Public Relations Failure. In the process of deposing Saddam, we placed our new seat of power right on top of his old one, just as the ancient Sumerians built their strongholds on top of fallen ones out in the desert. In addition to the new buildings, Saddam's old palaces in the Zone were repurposed as offices, and Saddam's old jails became our new jails. Conveniently for Iraqis, the overlords might have changed but the address had not. The place you went to visit political prisoners who opposed Saddam was still the place you went to look for relatives who opposed the Americans.

The new Embassy compound isolated American leadership at first physically and soon mentally as well. The air of otherworldliness started right with the design of the place. American architects had planned for the Embassy grounds to have all sorts of trees, grassy areas, and outdoor benches; the original drawings made them look like a leafy college campus. For a place in the desert, the design could not have been more impractical. But in 2003 no projection into the future was too outlandish. One building at the compound was purpose-built to be the international school for the happy children who would accompany their diplomat parents on assignment. It was now used only for offices. Each Embassy apartment offered a full-size American range, refrigerator, and dishwasher, as if staffers might someday take their families to shop at a future Sadr City Safeway like they do in Seoul or Brussels. In fact, all food was trucked in directly from Kuwait, along with American office supplies, souvenir mugs, and T-shirts ("My Father Was Assigned to Embassy Baghdad and All I Got Was . . ."; "I'd Walk a Mile for a Camel") and Embassy staff members were prohibited from buying anything to eat locally. The Embassy generated its own electricity, purified its own water from the nearby Tigris, and processed its own sewage, hermetically sealed off from Iraq.

The Ambassador, who fancied himself a sportsman, ordered

grass to grow on the large sandy area in front of the main
Embassy building, a spot at one time designated as a helicopter
landing zone, since relocated. Gardeners brought in tons of dirt
and planted grass seed. A nearly endless amount of water was
used, but despite clear orders to do so the grass would not
grow. Huge flocks of birds arrived. Never having seen so much
seed on the ground in one place, they ate passionately. No grass
grew. The Ambassador would not admit defeat. He ordered
sod be imported into Kuwait and then brought by armored
convoy to the Embassy. No one confessed to what it cost to
import, but estimates varied between two and five million dollars. The sod was put down and hundreds of thousands of gal-
lons of water were used to make it live, in what was practically
a crime against nature. Whole job positions existed to hydrate
and tend the grass. No matter what Iraq and nature wanted,
the American Embassy spent whatever it took to have green
grass in the desert. Later full-grown palm trees were trucked in
and planted to line the grassy square. We made things in Iraq
look the way we wanted them to look, water shortages throughout the rest of the country be damned. The grass was the
perfect allegory for the whole war.

The efforts were not wasted, as the Ambassador organized
an Embassy lacrosse team to gambol on the lawn. At one point
the official Web site featured photos of young Iraqis receiving a
donation of Major League Baseball equipment on the turf. The
event was a special program the Ambassador was personally
involved with, because he believed in "sports diplomacy." Once
he invited Iraq's only baseball team to his residence for some
drills. He wore a replica of a Japanese-born Major League
star's jersey, making the point that baseball, although invented
in America, was an international sport (which is why the World

Series includes only American teams and potentially a Canadian one). "Baseball is like democracy," he liked to say, "you cannot impose it. People should learn it and accept it."[32] A previous sports diplomacy program donated hundreds of soccer balls to Iraq, each colorfully decorated with flags of the world. No one would play with the balls, because they included the flag of Saudi Arabia, which has a Koranic verse on it, and you cannot put your foot to a Koranic verse. Luckily, the balls were made in China, where they already knew not to include the Israeli flag, as it would have been awkward if we'd had to ask.

Most of the State people at the Embassy were not me or my kin. While the various job specialties in the military (mortar plate carrier and helicopter pilot, cook and General) were united by a single uniform, a common service affiliation, and an esprit de corps, the State Department was more of a confederation, where lines were rarely crossed. If my kind were strip malls, the people here were Galleria.

The traditional diplomat was a big part of the organization and provided most of the upper management. While diversity played its role, this group was still mostly male, pale, and Yale in orientation if not in actual appearance. They were the deep thinkers, the plotters, the negotiators, the report writers. These folks, the ones the media always refer to as attending receptions wearing striped pants (striped pants went out of style with Hoover although many State officers have hung on to bow ties, seersucker, and men's hats), were content in their Iraq assignments, as their work involved staying in the Embassy and sending important memos to one another and to Washington, nipping out occasionally for chats with ex-expat Iraqis imported and perhaps even test-tube-bred by us for such purposes. Upper management types created their own reality and walled it off from the rest of the country. Army joke: How does the Embassy keep an eye on events in Iraq? From the roof.

Coming into the Embassy from the field was one of the more stressful things you could do in Iraq, made worse if you drifted into Baghdaddy's, the Embassy bar. You began to understand why Embassy policy forbade photography at after-work events once you learned that the most important characteristic of Baghdaddy's was that booze was cheap. You bought a punch card for twenty dollars and drank and drank, as all the bartenders were volunteers from the Embassy community and free drinks, heavy pours, and loose accounting were the norm. The serious drinkers rolled in right at 8:00 p.m. to start on two-dollar shots of vodka, grain, or maybe kerosene. These were the older, former alpha males of the community, no longer able to attract mates and shorn of their once proud plumage, who just wanted to get drunk rapidly with purpose. Eight o'clock was like the VFW hall on a pale Wednesday afternoon—if you were there, you were there to drink, and if you were drinking, you wanted to get shitfaced. If you wanted to talk to anyone, you'd drunk-dial your ex-wife.

The next phylum slid in around ten, the twenty-to-thirty-year-old Embassy staffers. They all knew one another and liked to dance and have a good time, basking in their youth and coolness and self-importance. Baghdaddy's was not Wisconsin Avenue in Georgetown, but with a popped collar on a pink polo shirt, a mixed drink in a DayGlo color, and sunglasses indoors, there was no reason why it couldn't be undergrad glory days all over again. Life in Iraq was no more real for these people than it was for anyone else dragging slowly through a one-year tour, but it was better dressed.

Things started to turn seriously sad around 11:00 p.m.

Older women drifted through the door in twos and threes, with the occasional grim single. They eased on strappy sandals to take advantage of the Embassy's 800 to 1 ratio of men to women. The odd dance between the older females and the game thirty-year-old undergrads would be pathetically interrupted by the stirrings of the now drunken former alphas, clumsily trying to make conversation while pushing aside the young challenger bulls from the kill site. Natural selection was not a pretty sight.

The world's worst bar scene ended when the overhead fluorescents jerked on at midnight, trapping the unsuccessful hunters in the glare. Quick words were exchanged on the dance floor in desperate attempts to seal a deal, while the serious boozers retreated to preaching from their stools and a final drink. Back in the room, late-night TV offered little solace, with an Islam Gigante Lebanese dancing show interrupted by nearly constant commercials for a Middle Eastern product called Pif Paf. Like an elderly widow who avoids dining with other aging women, knowing loneliness shared is only loneliness multiplied, Baghdaddy's made everyone grow apart, while maintaining the illusion of bringing them together.

Economic Conference Blues

If bullshit were water, we'd all drown, so take a deep breath. A couple of days at the Embassy for an economics conference left my head spinning. The participants were the usual pickup team that runs the war's civilian side: slick 3161 job shoppers, retired thises, a former that, and a few once-wases, people who incestuously briefed one another—all of the facts, none of the understanding, the big picture, our "legacy." The new adjective of choice was *robust*. Iraqi Americans increasingly figured on the team, some remembering Baghdad from their youth, most still struggling with English, but all empowered to spend, spend, spend—money is a weapons system. So much cash in play, there's a new slang word in Iraqi Arabic, *duftar*, a tall pile of Benjamins totaling $10,000. Ka-ching!

A session on car loans, a new front to spur the economy, but a challenge: Iraq has no repo law. A name needed for a bridge in Diyala, "American Freedom Bridge" our choice, a plaque to be bought. USAID briefs, gonna spend $82 million to strengthen government-provided health care. Forward movement, money equals progress, activity is achievement, $60 million to revive the financial sector, most definitely time to form a bankers' association so there's someone to work with. Will plan webinars and roundtable discussions, maybe a blog, oh yes, a blog is modern, get an intern on it, they know this online stuff.

State up next, tells us we must double down on our government of Iraq partners, help them spend Iraqi money on reconstructing Iraq, take the R out of PRT, and make the locals pay, spend, spend, spend, volume the key to success. Create chambers of commerce to facilitate investment, maybe with a nice brochure, the lack of a chamber the last obstacle on the road to prosperity. Quick bright things come to confusion, said Shakespeare. Don't slow down. Integrate. Act, engage, facilitate, mentor, promote, task, develop. There are no problems just challenges and issues. Security is an issue; a guy murdered in front of his family a challenge to stability. Language employed to keep thought at bay, said Pinter.

Task one: Suspend disbelief, rewire your brain, accept that people at the Embassy who never stray outside the Green Zone tell you about Iraq, the place you live 24/7. Safety improving, suicide bombings down, democracy up, cognitive dissonance not a problem, you can't really tell but we're winning (the preferred narrative of the war). From the head PRT office, "Due to security concerns, we are unable to visit the Baghdad Flower Show, which the Mayor intended to be a symbol of stability."

Task Two: Convince yourself of the overall premise of the US efforts, that Iraqis want to be like us. They want to have banks like us, farms like us, governance like us, repo laws like us, fast food, rock and roll, MTV like us. Hire Iraqis who see it our way, find young women who change from *hijabs* into club wear on campus, happy natives to confirm our visions in the heat. Enjoy the Kool-Aid, sweet even when it is bitter.

Much crowing over success in persuading Craigslist to add a page for Iraq—http://baghdad.craigslist.org—most sections not used (it is in English), still definitely a step to economic growth. Rabbit-quick checked my computer (sweet, sweet Wi-Fi here), lots of Men Seeking Men personals, military-age male Americans looking for boy sex in Iraq. Some wanting other gay men, some offering themselves as expedient alternatives in Iraq ("My mouth can replace her pussy"). A few sad posts from heteros hoping there are women out here who want them bad enough to troll Craigslist. A fifty-two-year-old gay man in Chicago, explicit photos, thanks all for their service, wants to correspond with muscled gay soldiers, patriotism, don't tell that he asked.

New briefer, just in from Washington, pretty junior, given the spot right before lunch when no one was interested in another rap. Things slowed down. She said that Iraq ranked 175th out of 180 countries as the hardest place in the world to start a business, that illiterates and high school graduates command about the same salaries because most hiring is for government patronage jobs (maybe 60 percent of everyone employed in Iraq now works for the government, no one knows). Most people in the room looked away, embarrassed for her for not getting the memo. She offered a formula to explain it all: Corruption = Monopoly + Discretion − Accountability. She believed the social fabric of Iraq is now in "survival mode." Woooh, awkward, suicide right on the stage. We exchanged glances, some signifying fear of agreeing, most shock over the heresy; she'd be reeducated. Conference organizers hit 911, rushed into the breach with a quick lunch, club sandwiches with crunchy bacon, then ice cream from Baskin-Robbins, brought in from the States, because we could. Back on track, no mind to the interruption, jury should disregard the last witness.

Next up, tourism briefing. This could be a big thing, says some reservist who was handed the portfolio as his way to fight the war. US government spent $700,000 in Babylon to build restrooms and a gate near the ruins, $300,000 to create the Baghdad Tourism Institute, $2 million for the Habbaniyah Tourist Village, to include $698,000 for beach refurbishment, literally paying for sand in Iraq (not the first time: my ePRT already bought Turkish sand to use in water filters). Guy says in 2009 sixty-five Western tourists visited Iraq (including eighteen Taiwanese, stand-in Westerners, and seventeen Americans). US Army polled them, learned they loved Iraq but hated the hotels, hoping to attract more next year. United States not much involved in the five to seven million Shia religious tourists who visit Iraq each year, kinda ceded that market to Iran, we'll focus on those sixty-five Westerners. Good news: US Army will spend $100,000 to fly in a hundred travel agents from around the world (including from Iran and this time Japan) for "Iraq Tourism Week" in early October. Market looking up for tourism, for sure, for sure.

Last briefing: Foreign Commercial Service will hold a "trade mission," charging US companies $6,000 to meet Iraqi businesspeople. The $6,000 includes a personal security detachment (good value), but you'll need to stay at the al-Rasheed Hotel, an additional $300 a night, plus pay for your own meals, US cash only, please. Brochure has the word *business* misspelled, oops, pointed that out to the guy, he wasn't happy with me, says they already sent out two hundred copies. Brochure also does not list the dates of the trade mission, security concerns, *ssshhh*, in October. Foreign Commercial Service briefer admits he has not been outside the Green Zone but relies on an Iraqi New Zealander to make contacts.

Final notes: good conference overall, a lot to take back, not much to remember.

Spooky Dinner

While the Army buzzed with adolescent energy, the Agency was all about cool. Cool as in "we got this, it's all taken care of." You didn't see much of them in Iraq, even though they were everywhere, as this wasn't really their war. Afghanistan was theirs at first, when a bunch of spooks with sat phones and blocks of greenbacks won the damn thing at least once, maybe twice, until what they call the GWOT (G-WOT, Global War on Terror) and the hunt for UBL (Usama bin Laden, always with a *U*—they knew bin Laden when you were still roller-discoing) were canceled midseason. That torqued the spooks off, because Afghanistan was their hood, their finest hour, where they had beaten the Red Motherfucking Army, without breaking a sweat, really, never mind that last bit about creating a worldwide armed, seasoned radical Muslim uprising; a bad bounce, for sure, but there was always some collateral. Hanging with these guys was a quick jolt of anticynicism medicine, steroids for the blackened soul, because they were all masculine confidence and certainty, brother, and it was infectious. Sure, the war may have been all about oil, but these dudes knew that a foreign policy based on fear—Japs, communism, terrorists— was what really kept the game alive.

It had been a long econ conference at the Embassy, a pep rally to make sure the ePRTs were with the program. Meanwhile, demonstrations protesting the lack of electricity had been popping up around Iraq. People had suffered in the swarming heat, 120 degrees if you could find a thermometer that went that high, without juice to run the AC or power to run the water pumps. The Embassy, living on corporate truth, was telling the world that power generation exceeded pre-2003 levels but that a rise in demand had resulted in a temporary gap that was most certainly not our fault. Of course, measuring life now against life pre-2003 had a tendency to downplay the billions spent for tiny gains, if any, and the thousands dead for nothing. The clever part was blaming the problem on demand (it's the damn Iraqis' fault). Truth inside the Green Zone: we're doing our job, power is up. Bottom line outside the Zone: two to six hours a day of power, delivered unpredictably. People dying, hospitals closing, and kids drinking river water, then spending a week horizontal, dehydrated from the runs. But check the PowerPoint and damn if it wasn't true, we *were* winning.

So why not celebrate? The Agency had arranged just the thing: a dinner at their compound. It was just like them not to list it on the schedule, OPSEC above all. Nobody was in the mood for more corporate culture that night, but secretly we all got off a little on the idea of hanging with the spooks on equal terms.

Despite our one-billion-dollar Embassy, with more security and walls around it than Mordor, the Agency had to set themselves up in a separate compound. They might have had some staff sleep in the Embassy apartments, maybe dump a few junior officers there as liaisons during the day, but when Daddy needs to do Daddy things, he can't be sharing the executive washroom with the Army or—God, no—even worse, State.

The Agency compound was a symbol for them of how this damn war was supposed to have worked out, taking control from the dictator in the most obvious way. The Agency grabbed for itself one of Saddam's primo palaces, in the Green Zone, of course, but separate from the Embassy and the Army. Saddam had palaces everywhere, practically one for everyone in the immediate aftermath of the invasion, before hangers-on like the Department of Agriculture, for Christ's sake, had come out to play. The Agency snatched up a good place and, with the balls they liked to believe they carried in wheelbarrows in front of them, had not altered it much. Outside they had thrown up T-walls and barriers and checkpoints and enough razor wire to encircle Folsom, perimeter security so that any yahoo driving past would know this was a serious place, not some random Army IT office or a goddamn State Department motor pool. No signs, of course, but hey, the real operators always know one another anyway.

The best parts were inside, where most of Saddam's I'm-on-crack decorating style had been left untouched. You could blink and think you were in a Macao sauna or Sinatra's Vegas for all the red velvet and brass, but the tacked-up strings of lights around the doorway and the big sign pointing to the bar as if you were in a frat house were giveaways for anyone who had been in any station anywhere. The pool with the winged griffin statues and red spotlights added to, but was not needed to complete, the scene. If you had ever gotten stoned as a kid, this was the vision you'd have wanted to stretch out your buzz.

But the Agency didn't do dope, it did booze. You would never imagine the Rat Pack with a hookah full of Panama Red, and you could not imagine anything but good whiskey and maybe some decent imported beer for this party. The Agency guys, used to being all hush-hush under the covers around State during daylight hours, loved these parties where they could (in their minds) blow our minds by introducing themselves by their actual titles. Of course, even in a large official community most people who cared pretty much knew who was who anyway, but certain things were not spoken out loud, so the titles were a big deal. You were supposed to feel that you were being given a peek behind the curtain and were meant to behave appreciatively. Most of us knew the protocol and things went smoothly.

I'd met one of the spook guys on another assignment and he was for real. Because we recognized each other and because this was a social affair, he was obliged to make a little conversation with me. Unlike some of his colleagues, who only looked cool around us until their moms called them home for dinner, this guy had been part of some of the big ops his Agency had run in the 1980s and 1990s. Tall and lanky, he had worked in Afghanistan—everyone of his generation had—but also in Mogadishu and some places I won't even type the names of. He could tell stories for hours but didn't, because in general your questions would be too damn stupid and he neither cared enough nor wanted to be nice to you. Yeah, sure, he'd say, that's how it was, like *Black Hawk Down*, but he said it in a way that let you know it was never like that. I asked what he was up to in Iraq just to see if he'd bother with a witty reply, but he didn't, just said, "You know, the usual." If you're posted somewhere and he shows up, you should probably leave, it's that simple. You're in too deep whether you realize it or not (you won't realize it). Most people believe either that the United States has thousands of officers like this named Bourne or Bond or that they don't exist except in the movies. But they are real, though there are not many of them and yeah, you're glad they're probably on the same side as you.

The Agency was quiet in Iraq because, as I said, this wasn't their war. They had nailed their biggest coup early on, still said to be controlling most of the budget for Iraqi intelligence. To them, holding the money meant that they were running the Iraqis though, as we knew, spending money in Iraq did not always mean control and sometimes the project turned and ran *you*. Like us believing we were building democracy and capacity in Iraq, the spooks believed they had a handle on the intel. The chances were good we were both equally deceived, the difference being we sort of knew it, if we cared to look at our reconstruction projects, while the truth about the spooky ops might take a decade and some congressional hearings to come out.

But this evening was about current success, not future failure, and the highlight came early as the host announced that the china and the silver we were eating with had been Saddam's and the table we sat at had been Saddam's and the room we were in had been His. Saddam had been a badass, but we had taken him down and the proof was in front of us: we got his stuff. If the Station Chief had told us he was wearing Saddam's old clothes, we would have believed him. Now, a cynic might point out that years had passed since we'd nabbed Saddam and that we hanged him in 2006 about a mile from where we sat, but this wasn't the night for it and we all took a moment to marvel at the plates and ask the person next to us what, if the room could talk, he thought it might say. Had Saddam deflowered virgins here, planned the invasion of Kuwait, and maybe met with al Qaeda right at this table, who knew? It was, of course, equally possible that in this room Saddam had met his Agency handlers in 1983 to discuss the war against Iran or receive info from Don Rumsfeld about the new weapons he was getting from the United States to kill Persians and Kurds. But like I said, the evening was about success and we ate rare steak and sipped good whiskey and allowed ourselves to absorb a little bit of the freshly squeezed juice of faith.

The Day after
a Day at the Embassy

We felt like hoboes, the four of us from the ePRT, walking around the Embassy compound after the economics conference. Almost everything was a contrast to the world we lived in. Nothing was dusty, nothing covered with the fine tan silt that defined our Iraq. The air-conditioning was silent and even—smooth, cool air that we sought to draw into our pores and take back to our FOB. The gleaming cafeteria always amazed us, from the sign apologizing for the Caesar salad station being temporarily closed to the surprisingly awkward, heavy feel of metal utensils (we used plastic, as if we were on a 365-day picnic) to the shock of a fruit-carving station stocked with fresh watermelon and papaya (we enjoyed those radioactive-orange-colored canned peaches in heavy syrup, more rumor than actual fruit). Unlike at the FOB, where the quality of the food made one thrifty about filling a plastic tray, we all loaded our china plates with fresh vegetables and crispy fries and ordered up

Slurpees (choice of four flavors) and coffee drinks lush with real cream and sugar. It was all free, take as much as you wanted, here at Club Fed. The only surge in sight was in cholesterol.

At the Embassy, the men who held pointlessly long meetings with us sported bow ties and pressed linen pants, while the women wore earrings and perfume. No one was armed, civilians outnumbered uniformed military 20 to 1, there were water fountains in the hallways and marvelous real flush toilets that did not smell of the persons who used them before you. We rode an elevator for the only time in Iraq. We were like children raised by wolves, now among those who should have been our own kind yet weren't.

When you saw an American woman on the FOB, she was usually a soldier, dressed in military clothing designed to hide body shape better than any *hijab*—one size fits no one, never a sense of, say, the lines of a summer dress hinting at the presence of her body. At the Embassy, you saw women in high heels, women in pants so impossibly tight that you died a little inside just to look; an employee imported from one of our embassies in South America wore black jeans and a yellow knit top with a black demi bra that stood out in bas relief. It might have looked crude in some universe, but here it was poetry, Old Testament–style temptation. Her body would leave an impression on history. Religions had been founded on less. The four of us looked like sad, desperate travelers from Mars as we stared.

A key aspect of our Sharia lifestyle on the FOB was the absence of alcohol, ostensibly banned by the military so as not to offend our Muslim hosts. But the Embassy knew no such restriction and the convenience store sold shampoo, magazines, cleaning supplies, and acres and acres of booze. You pushed through the swinging door to cases of cheap Budweiser, crates of Heineken, and every kind of liquor, liqueur, spirit, wine, and hooch known to man. Four varieties of flavored Grey Goose, Johnnie Walker in every color (including a $150 bottle of Blue), and types of vodka and gin I never knew existed. We stood there in air-conditioned comfort and browsed until the mere sight of it all made us inebriated, and only then did we carry our choices to the cash register, where we paid by credit card. A credit card, here at war! The wonder of it all wore off quickly given humans' astonishing ability to adjust, so we had to grab at each sensation and catalog it before it became part of our new evolving normal, as ordinary soon as the Embassy's Pizza Hut, the Starbucks clone Green Bean, the indoor swimming pool, the sign advertising swing dance lessons on Tuesdays, the Wi-Fi in the lounge, the lounge, the bar, the magazines published within the last two months, the hair salon that did highlights, the misters spraying cool water into the air to allow people to sit comfortably outside, the tennis courts, the driving range—all dizzying reminders that we Americans were strangers, useless to the needs of the place.

At the helipad, waiting for our ride home, we sat around for ninety minutes until it got dark enough to take off. Even with GPS, a lot of helicopter navigation is done by eye as the pilots try to avoid wires and land on small pads at remote installations. The pilots can fly easily in the daylight, and easily in the dark with night-vision gear, but it is tricky in the in-between times.

Darkness had new meaning here. Unlike in the States, where there were almost always some lights on, in the desert, when the moon was not out, you could not see your own feet beneath you. To better use their night goggles, the pilots blacked out the helicopter and switched off their outside lights. Flying this way was oddly therapeutic, as there was nothing to see, there were no reference points, just the enveloping sound of the helo and the comforting sensation of motion. We flew in a UH-1, the Vietnam-era helicopter everyone knows from the movies, which had a tendency to slide through the air in a series of long, lazy curves. Finally, we saw the lights that marked our home helo pad. The lights were not bright airport beams but small Chem-Light dots at the corners of the landing zone, almost invisible to the naked eye but nice and clear with night goggles.

We had to move by feel once on the ground. Vulnerable to mortar attack, the pilot was in a hurry to get airborne again. I got out of the helo and the crew chief, whose job it was to load and unload us, also jumped out to make sure I walked away properly. Because it was so dark, it was easy to get disoriented, and walking into the spinning tail rotor blades was death. The crew chief had night goggles and usually gave everyone a push from behind to get them moving in the right direction. Somebody eventually flashed a dim light to guide you. Not so easy, but you got used to it. This time the crew chief sent my colleagues off the LZ but held me by the shoulder and shouted that I was to wait for a soldier with a lot of gear to get out and then help him carry the load.

Suddenly the helicopter engine engaged and the crew chief grabbed me by the jacket sleeve and jerked me backward onto the ground as the helo took off. The tail rotor spun over our heads and the bird disappeared with a roar into the black sky. There was no quiet like the hole left when a helo departed, the noise so powerful suddenly withdrawn. We were flat on the ground, with stuff spread all over by the downward blast of the rotors. Had the crew chief not flung me and himself down, we would have been killed. Dead without knowing it, just like that, dear Mrs. Van Buren, the Department of State regrets to inform you . . .

It was a rough way to break free from the Embassy cocoon, where their ignorant eagerness for things as they wanted them to be ran head-on into our thoughts about things as they were. We had not always gotten along, the four of us from the ePRT, arguing over the right thing to do, the best way to spend our money and get through our year. Still, though I was a bit in shock from the helo incident and scared after the fact, I was happy to be back with my teammates in the more familiar world of the FOB. Regrouped, we moved gracelessly to a small patio near our office outlined by a Conex shipping container on one side, a sloppy brick wall standing because it was too lazy to fall on a second, and the remnants of another building on the third. Usually when we came back with our secreted beer from the Embassy, we parceled the cans out in ones and twos, trying to make the stash last longer, like teens in our parents' basement. A can tonight, maybe two on Friday, and a couple of cases could pass the time for weeks. Tonight something unspoken made us greedy. We chugged cans, we popped the tops of the ever-warmer brew (room temperature was 104 degrees), and slurped the foam like Vikings on a New World bender. One of the benefits of not drinking often was that your body dried out, and so even a little alcohol thrown down that dry hole kicked your ass. A lot of alcohol drunk purposely under these conditions sent four adults into drunkenness marvelously rich and fine. It tasted of a high school June.

With a lot of dust in the air and only a toenail-clipping-shaped moon out, the darkness was complete as we sat drinking the last beers. A light would have embarrassed us. Seen in a photo, we could have been anywhere; there were no clues for an outsider to decode. We four felt closer to this place, and to one another, than we ever had.

The long days at the Embassy, where we had been laughed at as Muggles, unworthy, the warm beer, and the blanket of the dark led to stories. With the exception of a long, wandering tale that had something to do with a tree, the Germans, and a lawsuit, we had all heard the drunken stories before. The two divorces, a daughter who did not write, the woman whose name had been forgotten even as the teller spent ten minutes describing how her shoes looked next to his bed—the stories all poured out in equal measure to the booze we poured down our throats. Some were bitter (the sum of our ages totaled over two hundred), most more matter-of-fact. A lifetime of experiences, a thousand autumns, all tied up in those voices.

We realized, maybe for the first time, that we had more in common than we had differences. Like every dog year equaling seven human ones, time spent together in Iraq fast-forwarded how you felt about the people sharing it with you. Nobody cursed Iraq—on the contrary, though none of us could walk a straight line to save his life, we were sharply aware that it was only because we were in Iraq that we could share what we were sharing. There was little talk of the routines of home that used to govern our lives: mortgages, Saturday morning chores and errands. That happened only at the beginning of your time, when you could still smell home on your shirt, or at the end of a tour, when you had to will yourself to remember so you could fit back in. The talk instead was about people, friends, lovers, girlfriends, wives, dads—what we did not have here and for whom we all accepted one another as surrogates. Maybe because we were drunk, we recognized we cared about one another, our differences not resolved but perhaps less vital. We hoped it would all end better than it probably would.

The next morning I awoke with a vicious headache and the realization that someday I would come to miss being with those men as much as I now missed the smell of pillows on my bed at home or kissing my wife when we both tasted of coffee. It was already over 100 degrees, a Thursday.

Soldier Talk

As the reconstruction suits had their meticulously chosen but empty terms such as *capacity building* and *Lines of Effort*, the troops had their own language and it always came as a welcome change. Playfully obscene, sneeringly in-your-face, it was a way of drawing in others who knew the language while politely excluding the rest. Sometimes it was spat out in the terse tones of an order, other times it was streaming commentary as the soldiers made fun of one another and their world.

I got a crash course in soldier talk over the internal headset communication system inside Army vehicles. On many of our drives to and from project sites we were alone on rural roads and had no need to give or receive orders. To pass the time, the soldiers entertained themselves with conversations that did not start and end but instead picked up a thread left dangling from the last mission, from lunch, from a conversation started a day ago.

CORPORAL WEISS: That dude can bench like 375, no shit.

LIEUTENANT ORTIZ: Don't hit that fucking dog up there.

CORPORAL WEISS: Why not, fucker is half lame anyway.

LIEUTENANT ORTIZ: You hit it, I'll fuckin' make you clean that fucking shit up.

Fucker is probably some kinda al Qaeda dog. Clear left?

Yeah, go ahead.

You seen the Staff Sergeant the other day?

No, what?

Fucker was all fucking high speed, like he was gonna dump the dismounts at some fricking railroad tracks.

Why?

Watch that.

OK, I fuckin' see it.

You didn't fuckin' see that garbage can you hit yesterday, asshole.

Like I was sayin', he said we had to see if we could cross but I told him we fucking crossed the other fucking day.

Yeah, fucking White is always like, "Watch that guy on the road, he got a cell phone, he could be triggering an IED," like every motherfucker in Iraq ain't got one.

That's it. He's all like, "He wearing a red shirt, and he got blue sandals, and he speaking Spanish" or some shit like it matters what the description says.

Check the radio.

LT, man, I just did.

I said check the fucking radio.

Falcon X-Ray, Red Cap One, Red Cap One, over.

I bought my wife like eight dozen roses online.

What the fuck for?

'Cause of our anniversary.

Red Cap One, this is Falcon X-Ray, send it, over.

Falcon X-Ray, Red Cap One, radio check, over.

You see the game last night?

No, my fucking hajji shop TV is fucked up again.

Fuckers cheat you.

Red Cap One, Falcon X-Ray, read you five by five, over, out.

No, why the fuck did you buy eight dozen fucking roses?

'Cause I thought they'd come from some real flower shop, you
    know, and some dude'll bring 'em up to the door, but instead
    they came from some shit-ass factory and they showed up in
    like eight boxes and she had to put them together herself.

No, asshole, why'd you buy eight dozen? How much did they cost?

'Cause I tried to click twelve but ended up with eight.

Dipshit motherfucker can't freakin' count.

Three hundred bucks.

I'd only fuckin' spend that on my girlfriend.

I'd fuck your girlfriend.

Like she would do you, no way. Checkpoint.

Where?

Up there by that rusted car.

Fuckin' Iraqis, man, everything is shit here. Why we gotta stay
    'til fucking December LT?

Watch your three o'clock.

I got it. Ain't nothing.

Shit, look out for that little kid on the left.

I fuckin' see her, shit.

You tried that Iron Man shit? Dude, get with the Sergeant Major, he got a video of it. Run a mile, then like fifty pull-ups—

I seen it, there was some chick in that video, right?

Yeah. She was like 120 pounds and she lifting like eighty-eight pounds fuckin' forever.

She was wearing that blue spandex shit, right?

You think of anything but fucking? You a fucking freak, man. Even the train it stop sometimes. Shit, turn up there.

Where?

After that ditch, shit for brains, on the same fucking Route Fatboy where we always fucking turn.

Roger, I got it LT.

LT was a shorthand way to refer to the lieutenant who oversaw the small group of soldiers who protected us while driving around Iraq. His mom and dad once gave him a name, but here he was just LT. He was rumored to have a sense of humor, but the job required that the LT's human side was on hold during the war. For example, when stopped near one of our projects off Route Fatboy, we saw a puppy, not more than a few weeks old, with no mama dog in sight. An enthusiastic debate opened up among the soldiers, with three wanting to bring the puppy back illegally onto the FOB (General Order Number One allowed for no pets) and two wanting to shoot the puppy and put it out of its misery. The debate ended with the LT saying, "We are not in Iraq to care about fucking puppies" and that was that. Another reason we were not fighting this war: it is not about puppies.

Route Fatboy was just one of the roads we commonly traveled on. Most roads in Iraq didn't have names, so as the US military created detailed maps, it supplied them. It was unclear how the process unfolded, but the results were Cheese Whiz American. Out in the area we worked, one set of roads named after stock car drivers connected to another named after heavy metal bands, which connected to a network named after beers. There was a road called Route Ricky Bobby, which merged with Earhart before becoming Fatboy. Take Route Fatboy for a while and you could turn off onto Incubus, then Slipknot, before reaching Metallica. Metallica was a straight shot north, but you could turn off at Bud, PBR, or Miller. In other areas, the roads were named after cars or, more romantically, women left behind, Betty, Marie, and Elizabeth by the older soldiers, Brittany, Tawana, and Carlita by the younger men. You heard it on the radio—"Gladiator Six, turning now onto Ricky Bobby, over"—and no one said the names ironically. Of course, no Iraqi knew who Ricky Bobby or Carlita was, so the road names also served as a kind of code.

In a cross between slang and officialese, the military made strange use of some words. I liked how they used the word *hasty*, as in "We set up a hasty perimeter" or "We chose a hasty defense," instead of *quick*, *casual*, or *sloppy*. You didn't see *hasty* used commonly otherwise except by George Will. I also liked how they used the phrase *get with* to mean talk with, work with, coordinate with, or check with, as in "SGT Ponds can help you. Get with her on that" or "Soldiers need to get with MED for redeployment checkups." *Kinetic* meant violent; a gunfight was kinetic, a tea party was nonkinetic. One soldier who served in Asia referred to snacks at a meeting as "licky-chewies." The Army still used all the old Indian fighting words—*troop, cavalry, saddle up*. The best was *guidon*, which could refer to the unit flag or the soldier carrying the unit flag. What other twenty-four-year-olds in America knew that word? The military also used a strange form of verb tense. They wrote, "Soldiers will not wear civilian articles of clothing in the gym" instead of "Soldiers may not wear civilian articles of clothing in the gym." It was as if the event had already not happened and the verb form described what already had not happened.

As in any other language, there were rules you had to follow to join the conversation. You never spoke about your spouse, kids, or pets by name. In soldier talk, names confused things. A guy had a girlfriend or a fiancée or a cat and that was that. The anonymity insulated you from troubling questions when the girlfriend left (Kristal was replaced by Shawna, still a girlfriend). No names allowed people to fudge the target of statements like "I am not believing I can't be with her for another eight months. I am going fricking crazy." Girlfriend? Wife? Who knew? But this way you could avoid violating another rule, speaking disparagingly of a current spouse or girlfriend. That was never done, and if you transgressed, the silence from your listeners slapped you across the face. It was permitted, however, to say pretty much anything about someone who had left you—cathartic for many and a challenge for the poets of profanity in our ranks.

When it came to talking about their profession, the soldiers would retreat to a set of clichés. Officers in particular seemed to need to repeat the same gung ho quotes over and over. They recited these tired lines to inspire at briefings and to perk up morale at meals and later memorialized them on plaques and fancy scrolls hung on the wall. My wish for when I left Iraq was never again to have to see or hear:

- Anything to do with Sparta.

- The phrase *blood and treasure*, as if we were paying for the war from a pirate chest overflowing with gold doubloons.

- The Teddy Roosevelt quote about the man outside the arena, that guy who knows neither victory nor defeat.

- Patton: "No bastard ever won a war by dying for his country. He won it by making the other poor dumb bastard die for his country."

- *Henry V*: "We few, we happy few, we band of brothers . . ."

- Jack Nicholson as Colonel Nathan Jessep to the court: "You can't handle the truth. . . . You want me on that wall, son. You need me on that wall."

Which led, finally, to this one, dubiously attributed to George Orwell: "People sleep peaceably in their beds at night only because rough men stand ready to do violence on their behalf." Different versions had those rough men standing on walls or "freedom's walls." But any which way, given that Orwell was no war lover, the quote sounded wrong. (It was. I looked it up: "He sees clearly that men can only be highly civilized while other men, inevitably less civilized, are there to guard and feed them.") Right or wrong, it lives on in a million e-mail signature lines.

Soldier talk needed to be negotiated around rank. Outside the FOB you could curse in front of an officer, while in the DFAC it was wise to start every sentence with "Sir" and keep it clean. The Sergeant who ran your squad might allow you to joke in some cases and demand a formal answer in others. Get it right and fit in, get it wrong and be labeled fresh meat. Civilians, lacking an explicit rank, confused the system and so some improvisation was required. One day, the main water pipe broke and everyone had to get in and out of the few working showers in ninety seconds. I must have stayed under the water too long, because the next man in line pounded on the door screaming, "Goddammit, get the hell out!" I heard someone say to him, "You can't say that, he's one of those State Department guys," to which the man responded, "Goddammit, get the hell out, SIR!"

Deep in the soldiers' language was a wry, sad humor that dispelled misery while acknowledging it existed. Almost nothing in this environment was in the soldiers' control, not where or how they slept, not what or when they ate or when they got shot at, and so almost everything was worth complaining about. Of course, everyone was experiencing the same misery, so complaints were often redundant, but they were permitted as an escape valve. Complaining was in fact a privilege allowed to long-suffering soldiers since Napoleon's time (*grognard*, meaning grumbler in French, came to mean an experienced combat vet). Complaining might build a kind of camaraderie. We could complain all the time, but then we would be sad all the time and that wouldn't be good. Better the bitching came out as a joke, a mockery, in great phrases like *Embrace the suck* or *Love the suck*. The suck was anything/everything wrong. On good days, such as frozen shrimpette night at the DFAC, people said, "We suck less tonight."

Sex

We all thought about it all of the time. A DJ flew in to play music as a morale thing. A blond nonsoldier woman with pneumatic breasts barely restrained by her T-shirt, the DJ thus attracted some attention. She was as comely as modern medical science could make her, her surgical enhancement a weird echo of the prosthetic limbs ubiquitous in this war. However, it was also 120 degrees outside and the DJ had set up in the sun on the shadeless basketball court, so even the most desperate soldiers stayed out only long enough to recharge their stores of fantasies. After two or three songs most soldiers realized she was not going to have sex with all several hundred of us, and the event ended up as dull as flat beer (also not allowed) that brought you nowhere but closer to the memory of better times and places.

In some of the small hajji shops on the FOB if you were a regular and things were, you know, cool, porn was available.

Most of it was cheap stuff with four-letter verbs as titles, though with some effort you could score professional filth from India, Asia, the Arab world, and of course the United States. Publicly, at least, the Army was a chaste organization, and while rampant DVD intellectual piracy was OK, looking at boobs was not. By order of Congress, the PX sold no *Playboy* or *Penthouse*. The naughtiest thing you could buy was *Maxim*, which sold out within minutes of restocking. The joke was that the Army once wanted to research the difference between soldiers who looked at porn and those who didn't. The problem was they couldn't find any men who did not.

Imagination was not prohibited, but General Order Number One in Iraq outlawed all other forms of fun: no cohabitation, no sex with locals, no booze, no pets, and none of anything else you might enjoy.[33] It was pretty thorough and lay like a wet blanket on top of a bunch of other military rules. For officers, adultery was an actual punishable crime, as, most likely, was dueling or having a handlebar mustache whilst commanding a cavalry charge. "Don't ask, don't tell" was also a rule of sorts in force at the time and was aimed right at sex. The Army loved its rules and, to be fair, needed some way to control the actions of so many people living so close to one another under wartime conditions. But as comprehensive as the rules were, in practice penning up a bunch of twenty-something soldiers, male and female, gay and straight, tired and active, tops and bottoms, exposing them to danger and then saying NO SEX, PLEASE worked about as well in the military as it worked in prisons, in college dorms, and at out-of-town sales conventions.

Sometimes it was sad. One female contractor, whose husband had unilaterally started divorce paperwork while she was still in Iraq, reacted by trying to sleep with as many married soldiers as possible. When word got to the Base Commander, he threatened to have her transferred until her employer balked, claiming she had essential technical skills needed to keep the computer network alive, and agreed to assign a 24/7 escort to keep her out of trouble. The Commander was responsible not only for the people on the FOB but also for the military spouses left behind. Word traveled fast between Iraq and the unit's base back home, and the Army was becoming more and more sensitive to winning the homecoming as well as the war. Jesus, it was hard enough for the Commander to read devastating blogs by twenty-year-old war widows, never mind having to assume responsibility for not busting up marriages.[34]

On any given night, as I took a walk hoping to get sleepy instead of just tired, I couldn't ignore the wet, sloppy sounds from behind nearby Hesco barriers. Latrines might be dirty and dark, but they also offered couples a bit of privacy. Liaisons were risky in a two-person trailer. A roommate could be bribed or begged to spend a little more time outside in sexile, but your neighbors might hear more than they cared to learn, and anyone could wander by and later decide to tell on you. One soldier acquired the keys to an empty CHU and shared his bounty with a lot of couples until a shower mishap put the soldier in a tough place—fess up to "borrowing" the keys or idly watch a broken pipe flood an entire daisy chain of sleeping quarters. He did the right thing, but the fun times ended after the KBR plumber ratted out the scam. If TDY meant "temporary duty" elsewhere in the world, in Iraq it stood for "temporarily divorced year." For those desperate enough, toilet graffiti remained a reliable advertising channel, and the requests were remarkably specific ("Eight-inch cut dude needs rough sex tonight behind gym"). It was human. It happened. A lot.

The biggest sexual adventure in our office was most note-
worthy as a failure. Even for a middle-aged man, our ePRT
colleague Harold had no game. Divorced equaled desperate in
Iraq, and you could almost smell it on him. After weeks of trying to chat up a young female Lieutenant in the gym, Harold
decided a nice e-mail inviting her for lunch would be just the
thing. He spent so much time composing the text that just
about everyone in the office had had a say in it. Most of us were
ready to ask her out for him to get the process over; high school
had gone smoother and quicker. Finally the e-mail was ready
and Cupid hit SEND. Harold waited. We all waited. Follow-
up strategies were discussed, and various reasons for the lack of
an immediate response were suggested as the clock ticked.

The first sign something was wrong was at the gym, where
said young Lieutenant began to appear not just in her somewhat
clingy regulation workout gear but also with a tall Captain who
seemed overly solicitous of her need for barbells and towels.
The signs were all there, but the floor did not fall out until
about three days later, when Harold's e-mail to the young Lieutenant, which she had forwarded to her not-so-best friend with
a snarky put-down was forwarded to the not-so-best friend's
friend with another remark about creepy old guys in the gym,
which was forwarded to a fourth person, who sent it on to most
of her company, who seemingly all had friends in Iraq (and
eventually Afghanistan). It took about a week before Harold's
simple, innocent words to the young Lieutenant morphed into
viral electronic statutory rape. Two snotty Facebook groups
were set up just to pass on the e-mail. One page offered "Harold's Pickup Lines" as contributed by fans: Do you want to
become the ultimate measure of my success in Iraq? Please date
me before the war ends. I really have nothing better to do so

would you like to go out? Let us start our enduring legacy today. Hey, baby, give me your e-mail address so I can ask you out in a lame way. I have diplomatic immunity . . . wanna wrestle?

As Harold begged us to bring him sandwiches so he could avoid stepping outside during daylight hours, the e-mail found its way to the Colonel who knew the solicitous Captain, who it turned out was now engaged (timing was everything in war) to the young Lieutenant. Things would have been bad enough for Harold had he not, in a fit of passion, mentioned in the same e-mail that he had "lots of free time to meet, even during the business day." That line reached the Embassy at the exact moment Harold's contract extension was up for consideration. The intersection of the ever-spiraling rumors that Harold had proposed treason, plus the tossed-off remark that he had a lot of free time, hit the poor guy right in the balls. The Embassy fired him and sent him back to the United States, where no doubt he lived not so happily ever after in the land of eHarmony.

As for Thomas in our office, it started with more curiosity than lust. Loneliness is a powerful thing; add to it some time for daydreaming and an atmosphere of 60 percent airborne testosterone and you start looking around. The woman who worked at the IT help desk, the one you saw a couple of times a week on business, what was she like? What did she do other than staple repair orders together? Did she ask those questions that seemed not work-related for some reason other than to pass the time? It was from there just a few short steps to saying the words "We should get coffee sometime," words that Thomas had not said to anyone but his wife for many years.

Coffee was purchased. Jokes were made about work. Common acquaintances were identified. Songs Thomas knew as anthems, the background sounds of his youth, she had maybe heard on an oldies station while driving her parents' car. She mentioned a few bands Thomas had never heard of; he tried to remember a group from anytime after 1985. She still hoped to read books Thomas had committed to understanding years ago. He had started a Facebook page to friend his children, while her page talked about the horses she hoped to own one day. They had no common background, only life histories hopelessly out of sync. Still, it was funny, it was exciting, it was forbidden with a big Do Not Touch sign. Unlike a wife, she represented not actuality but possibility. She was smart, there was paper there that had not yet been written on, and she was restless in a cocoon she wanted help in removing. They agreed that the food was terrible, that the weather was awful, that sometimes the public service announcements on AFN TV were funny, but mostly they agreed without saying a word that they were lonely and they were curious, and those were powerful things. Finally, it was dusk, which helped hide what they wanted to do.

Thomas kissed her, suddenly, and after that they fumbled together at unfamiliar Velcro on Army uniforms and civilian clothing that seemed out of place. It was a long way for Thomas from a high school dance when that first rayon bra strap had slipped off that first pale shoulder. But, like summer rain, the drops had been threatened for a long cloudy afternoon before the clouds broke open. After the storm the air was precious and sweet and simple, a watercolor of shampooed hair unbundled and Dial soap and the perfume of Army toothpaste and baby powder.

The overhead fluorescents, the only lights available when light was finally necessary, were harsh. The two realized lingering would make things more wrong than anything that had passed between them. Thomas never saw her again, the press of business being what it was, the Army moving people around as it does. In some moments alone he remembered what happened. She was pink, soft, and, well, new.

Later that night Thomas's wife e-mailed to say their youngest child was sick, had come home late from a party, was throwing up, and the washer was full of messed-up sheets. He told us he ran back to the office to Skype home, say a few words of encouragement, what a drag, hope she is OK, sorry he could not be there to help. He knew where he lived, he knew what he was, and he knew he had indeed left more behind now in Iraq than he could take home. Thomas was human, and it isn't always easy to be human. It happened. It was awful. It was wonderful, wonderful.

General Anxiety

Most of the troops were easygoing, officers and enlisted alike, accustomed to austere conditions and committed to making the best of things. Discipline was always present, and low-ranked soldiers needed to show respect for those above them, but under combat conditions what some would call bullshit was generally kept to a minimum. The exception was VIP visits, which required that the foot lockers full of bullshit be brought out from storage and opened for all to put to use.

General Anxiety, a four-star Army General prominent enough in real life to be referred to only by one name (like Bogart or Depp), was scheduled to drop by our FOB. Knowing the key to success of a VIP visit was massive quantities of food, our officers tasked four lower-ranked Army men, who no doubt joined the military to learn a useful trade, with laying out two trays of "wraps," along with significant donut assets. There was also a large plate of grayish hard-boiled eggs. Intel leaked that the General liked hard-boiled eggs, and so thirty eggs gave themselves up for hard-boiling. The Major in charge of refreshments ordered two soldiers to peel the eggs to spare the General the need to peel his own, wasting valuable General time. A large bowl with thirty peeled eggs was set in front of the General's seat. The Major decided that did not look right and ordered the soldiers to arrange the eggs on a plate. The soldiers tried to build a pyramid of hard-boiled eggs, failing repeatedly, until the Major ordered them to stop. The Major then determined that putting about ten eggs on the plate would be sufficient for the General's snacking needs, with the remainder of the eggs held in reserve. The men moved on to pile juice box after juice box on the table, such that each person faced about a gallon of artificial OJ, subdivided into tiny cartons. Of course, no one would touch any of the juice, in large part because the only way to drink it was through the attached straw, exactly as you did in fourth grade, and you looked like a dork. The Sergeant Major walked in to make sure everything was ready. Without saying a word, he moved the plate of peeled eggs off to a side table and replaced it with a carafe of coffee. He had heard the General liked coffee. He did not know about the eggs.

The General swept into the room like an unwelcome draft as everyone stood at attention behind their chairs. The General frowned and asked the Colonel to ask the Sergeant Major to ask the Corporal to ask the Private outside for a Diet Coke. The Colonel then pushed the coffee he usually drinks by the quart away and said he, too, would like a Diet Coke today. The Major in charge of refreshments went outside to organize this, not having anticipated two Diet Cokes in his snack plan. Nobody touched the eggs.

The briefing began as always, with PowerPoint. The value of PowerPoint to the military cannot be overstated; it is the only way many officers can communicate with one another. (Especially talented slide makers are known as PowerPoint Rangers, and in some shops you could buy a fake PowerPoint Ranger patch that mimicked the real Ranger tab earned with blood and sweat.) The history of using visual aids started back in the day with real photographic slides, then switched to viewgraphs in Vietnam until the 1990s, when PowerPoint arrived to save democracy. There were rules, of course. A military PowerPoint slide was not to include any white space. Something had to cover every micrometer of slide real estate, whether it was seven or eight fonts, star-spangled bullets, multiple underlining, type so small it's unreadable, layers of underexposed blurry photos, or, if you were in the company of pros, clip art. Assume, if the slide referred to a "soft landing," you'd get a stick figure with a parachute and that "Road Ahead" slides would include a stock photo of a highway stretching to an infinity point. The impression was 1990s GeoCities Web site, leavened with touches of a first Mountain Dew–fueled teenage Myspace page.

The long-established tradition was that, for every slide, the VIP would ask one question or make one comment to earn his entitlement to the snacks. The question had to be easily anticipated. If the slide showed four bullet points, the VIP would be expected to ask for more detail on one of them (four soldiers would be in attendance, each prebriefed on one of the four items). Two or more questions meant the VIP was looking for a fight. Most questions, however, were things like "Everything going OK for you with that project?" (yes) or "Anything I need to do for you from my side?" (no). A well-prepared VIP would come armed with his own laser pointer to highlight some element of each slide, while a well-prepared Colonel would be ready to hand over his own pointer to a visitor who forgot his.

At least one of the VIP comments would include (a) a personal story from the old Army (father-figure type), (b) a modestly naughty word (soldier's soldier), or (c) a saying such as "Winners never quit, quitters never win" (leader of men). Extra points for a sports metaphor that involved being close to the goal line (an astonishing 99 percent of today's sports metaphors were football-related). A few VIPs attempted to comment in a humorous way, heavily telegraphed so that everyone was ready to laugh on cue.

To me, the lone civilian at these events, they always felt like Bring Your State Department Guy to Work Day. My role was to be awed by the grown-ups, to sit up straight, not to touch anything, and to speak only when spoken to. Almost every VIP felt the need to acknowledge me, somewhat surprised that a nonuniformed person was allowed in the room. They would say, "Are you getting all the support you need?" like I was a houseguest needing extra towels. I would answer yes. I could have added another sentence, but no one was listening, because the point was to ask the question, not to listen to the answer. I could have asked for a back rub and skateboards and no one would have noticed.

After the PowerPoint slides and a few questions, the important people rushed out to the next event while the rest of us stayed and ate donuts. The eggs smelled sulfury and the Major threw them away.

Every so often we'd have a visit from nonmilitary VIPs like the gaggle of "fellows" who flew in from a prominent national security think tank. These scholars wrote serious books important people read, they appeared on important Sunday morning talk shows, and they served as consultants to even more important people who made decisions about this war and others to come. One of them was on the staff of a General whose name was dropped more often than Jesus's at a Southern Baptist AA meeting. Another was coming back to Iraq as an adviser to the Embassy, having advised in the glory days of 2003.

One guy was a real live neoconservative. A quick Google of his work showed he strongly supported going to war in Iraq, wrote apology pieces after no one could find any weapons of mass destruction ("It was still the right thing to do"), and came back to see exactly how well democracy was working out for a paper he was writing to further justify the war. He liked military high tech; he used words like *awesome, superb,* and *extraordinary* (pronounced EXTRAordinary) without irony to describe tanks and guns. He said in reference to the Israeli Army, "they give me a hard-on." Another fellow had a habit of bouncing his legs up and down while sitting. Strapped into the MRAP vehicle with the four-point harness that came up through his legs, he bounced and bounced, like something a dog did that embarrassed you when company came over. This guy basically advanced the thesis that anything that happened in Iraq before he started advising was a "fucking disaster" (it was so cool when academics used swear words) and whatever had happened after he started advising was "innovative." He insisted on using the phrase *tipping point* to refer to just about everything, including lunch. He called people in the news by their first names (Barack, Joe, Meatloaf). He looked at his smartphone for messages a lot, even though we were several hundred years away from the right kind of cell phone coverage.

The best thing of all was that when these two fellows were

together they did not talk about bands of brothers, Israeli wood, or Iraqi democracy, but instead, riding in an armored vehicle through the badlands outside of Baghdad, they compared book deals and literary agents and gossiped about people they both knew who were getting big advances on memoirs. It became clearer to me why this war had played out so well, with people like this intellectually backstopping the policy makers.

Waiting

Soldiers did a lot of waiting. They waited for orders, they waited for trucks to arrive, they waited for chow, they waited for someone to explain why they were waiting. Some of those waiting days were liquid. Like the plot of a bad Southern novel, the air started to feel heavy in the heat, and hours progressed immersed in thick sap. A lifetime passed between 11:42 and 11:57. Time was the main character in this story, because time was what we all had. Everyone had been here for so many days (newbies), weeks (didn't notice them so much), months (showoffs). Everyone had only so many days left (showoffs), weeks (too many to count down), or months (losers). You lived inside your calendar; you hated your calendar. Your time was owned by someone else. Not as bad as prisons, nursing homes, and shipwrecks, but it was an artificial way to live. Soldiers learned how to ingest time as if it were a physical thing. They became Zen masters of boredom, always waiting.

Everyone counted the days, almost from the beginning, when it seemed 365 steps away was forever (it was). I allowed myself to download a widget to count down how many days I had left in Iraq. Lots of people had one, but I had held off at first, hoping to mark time with my accomplishments, not just by scratching marks into the prison walls. My widget was a donut-shaped graph on my laptop, with time remaining in one color and time already spent in another. It seemed sad when I first installed it but I knew it would be cooler than hell by Day 298 (it was). One military contractor had a coffee cup he never washed, his way of counting. The cup went from stained brown to coated inside in brown goop. The owner claimed he could make passable coffee in the cup just by adding hot water.

Much of what separated the enlisted men and women from the officers was how much waiting they endured. The lower your rank, the earlier you had to show up for events and formations. Your waiting reduced the waiting an officer needed to do, like Jesus dying to take on someone else's sin. Waiting was worse for the many soldiers who never left the FOB, assigned to the hospital or the computer center. They spent their entire year in Iraq inside the walls, functioning in what could be considered a decent minimum-security prison or maybe low-rent assisted living, depending on how you viewed the quality of the food. Some Joes joked about video games, saying if *Call of Duty* wanted a truly realistic modern war experience, it would begin with a four-hour real-time wait in an airport followed by three days hanging around waiting for the paperwork to catch up with you before your character got assigned a boring desk job somewhere on base.

They waited, too, back home. We regularly had communications blackouts, when the Army cut off the Internet and the phones on the FOB. The blackouts lasted two or three days and were usually after a soldier was killed and the Army did not want anyone calling his or her family or the media or posting online until the next of kin had received official notification. For our spouses and children, panic set in when the e-mails and Skype stopped suddenly. They knew it meant someone had died, and they held their breath until they learned who. That was hard, so we usually figured out which one of us had a cell phone with international dialing that worked outside the Army system. There were a lot of ten-second calls to say the dearest words a soldier can utter to a waiting loved one, "Can't talk, but I'm OK."

The more you had at home to miss, the worse the waiting was. With the exception of a few true blues who found their family in the service and some of the older guys divorced enough times to just not care anymore, everyone else had someone at home they missed. In the old movies, mail call was a set piece—the moment when the tough but kind Sergeant called names and everyone went off to read their letters. In our war, communication was omnivorous-present, and waiting was done at Internet speed. Facebook did not exist when this war started (war, March 2003; Facebook, February 2004), but it sure as hell was here now. Even in the smallest dirt hole there was a sat phone or some kind of Internet connectivity or someone with the right Jetsons iPhone that got a cell signal in a place that did not even get daylight some weeks.

It started off as a good thing. We don't have to wait for the mail! Hey, I can call you from the war! This is so cool, OMG txting U frm iRaQ LOL. Sometimes it *was* cool. But a lot of times it meant two worlds that had nothing in common but the soldier collided. Why the hell was she Skyping from home about a small problem with the backyard fence when I've just come in from six hours in 110 degrees looking for an arms cache site? What to do about the leak in the basement? You call a plumber, burn down the house, I don't care, we just took a mortar round and I'm going to miss my only hot meal of the day in five minutes.

Other times it was worse. No one picks up at 3:00 a.m. back home in a house that is supposed to contain a sleeping wife. Kids answer the phone, distracted by the Disney Channel, and have nothing to say. You worry that the substitution of a phone call for a birthday party grows old even for weary preschoolers. The attempt to reconcile a life out here with a life over there fails again and again and again, until you quit trying. Yeah, the lines were down, or I guess you weren't home when I called, or maybe I'll call in a week or so or fucking never, bitch. Sometimes after they'd hung up you watched guys unable to say it earlier whisper "I love you" to the phone.

Of course, many nights it was different and you wanted to sit with the phone to your ear and hear the voice at the other end talk about anything, nothing, forever, your world collapsing into the wire. You clung to a wife complaining about the dry cleaner because that represented somewhere better than where you were and today your head was screwed on tight enough to realize it. You had to store up the good stuff when you could get it because you couldn't count on its coming when you needed it. Like sleep, you wished there was a way to bank it.

The availability of communication sometimes forced on me more than I wanted to accept. I was waiting to go home, waiting to hear from my child, waiting for my turn to use the phone, and had no strength left to share everyone else's burden. I walked past a stranger on the phone in the calling center and heard him say "I want to lick your pussy" to a girl somewhere else. I saw a man listening to a six-year-old recite lines from a play seven thousand miles and a world away, using the speakerphone so he had both hands free to cover his eyes. It was too much to be plunged this deeply into the lives of people I didn't know, and I wished at those times that phones and e-mail and Facebook and Twitter would just go away. Outside the calling center I saw an orange dot poking a hole in the darkness and smelled cigarette smoke. I heard another guy crying in the latrine, buttoned up into some of the only privacy available. He couldn't pick the moment for his breakdown—technology thrust it onto him. That's when I knew it was bad. I stopped sleeping for a while and started just waiting for my own mornings to come.

Everyone Was Looking
the Other Way

The ePRTs had morphed into a mechanized mode in spinning up new projects. There was not a lot of thought expended, as our instructions were the more projects the better. The Frankensteinian NGOs we had given life to so they could absorb our money had started coming to us directly with projects rather than waiting for us to call them. Our ePRT came up with an innovative idea: instead of these so-called NGOs approaching us and our staff doing all sorts of paperwork, why not have them simply ask for the money directly from the Embassy, removing us from the loop and cutting our workload to almost zero? We had not been doing any due diligence anyway, so why not take the whole process to the next level? We submitted a QRF (Quick Response Fund) grant request for $19,720 to teach NGOs how to request QRF money. We'd sit back and watch the circle complete itself. The original project:

Nascent NGO Training is designed to increase the efficiency and operational capability of newly formed NGOs.
The training will consist of training twenty-five NGOs
for three months. The NGOs will be required to write
proposals and, if approved for QRF, the projects will be
funded and implemented through the nascent NGO. The
training will be deemed successful if the QRF committee
approves twenty percent of the proposals.[35]

This was too much even for the usually roly-poly QRF committee, which torpedoed the idea, saying, "QRF cannot fund a
project to teach NGOs how to apply for QRF funding." The
ePRT edited the proposal ever so slightly, merely shuffling a few
paragraphs around in a way that would make a grade school
teacher reach for her red pencil, and resubmitted it. We didn't even
change the dollar amount. The embassy approved the project.

The budget:

Project manager	$3,000
Coordinator	1,500
Administrator	2,400
Trainer	4,800
Workers	600
Monthly reports	300
Rental of conference hall	3,600
Coffee, tea, snacks	1,200
Printing and copying	1,200
Certificates	500
Whiteboard	300
Flip chart	320

Who were all these people and what did they do? We did not know. We were offering great money for only three months' work; by comparison, the average yearly wage in Iraq was around $2,000, while a skilled worker might make $10 an hour. Good to see we were generous in providing $1,200 worth of tea and coffee. We paid the money out and hired a project manager. Training was said to have commenced. We sent a local employee one time to observe, but the NGO's guards (maybe they were the $600 workers we paid for?) prohibited her from entering the facility. I decided to make an unannounced visit to see our cash in action.

The trip brought us to another world, in this case an abandoned Saddam-era sports facility. We did not immediately locate any NGO classes but did attract the attention of the usual large group of kids and unemployed men who were everywhere in free Iraq, passing the time of day. They told us the slums we saw to the right used to be dormitories for Saddam's prized athletes, though squatters now occupied them. The squatters had run hundreds of wires from the nearest electrical poles, bringing pirated power into the complex. The lower floors of the buildings flowed with raw sewage, ripe in smell and buzzing with flies. The residents had walled off the former patios to make more room inside and had taken to throwing their household trash out the windows to collect in fetid piles between the buildings. It was 113 degrees, and the stench of garbage mixed with the heat in a bad way. A three-legged mutt growled, showed his teeth, and dug in, refusing to allow us to walk past. Knowing most strays in Iraq were rabid, we started to back away, as the soldiers with us primed their weapons. The impasse was broken by three shoeless boys who threw great chunks of concrete at the dog (one can guess what had happened to the fourth leg), scaring it away.

We passed a burned-out city bus, which the boys told us had been blown up years ago and now served as home for the feral dog pack. From time to time, the kids said, someone set fire to the bus and temporarily smoked out the dogs. A mother in full *abaya* poked her head out of an alley, a child on her hip, and yelled at us to leave. This was pretty gutsy, considering our group included seven armed soldiers, but maybe she had seen us back down from the three-legged dog. Our translator asked if there was a class somewhere nearby and she said some people had taken over part of the sports complex and had money, so maybe we should go there.

The sports complex was a short walk between garbage mounds away and could have easily been used as the set for the next *Terminator* movie. Here was the "conference hall" we had rented for $3,600. The floors were covered with sewage and almost every window was busted out. The hallways were filled with cats, dozens of them, and the walls were covered with giant drawings of musclemen posing, a Saddam touch. We saw light ahead and indeed it was the office of the NGO. Word had reached them that we were prowling around, and several people were frantically being frantic. Though it was after 10:00 a.m., there was no 9:00 a.m. class in session. We were told people were "late," and then, as if by magic, a dude in tight jeans showed up with a brand-new HP laptop and announced today's lesson would be about using the Internet. The frantically frantic people piled into the room and became the class. His Internet lesson seemed a bit contrived, as it consisted of his demonstrating how he logs on to Yahoo! Messenger, beginning with his writing the word *connect* in English for us on the $300 white-board.

The devolution of counterinsurgency into counterreality was hardly limited to my ePRT, or to the State Department. My sister PRTs and the Army contributed their share by funding guaranteed-to-fail small businesses like car washes and brake repair shops, in an economy struggling just to take a breath. Social engineering in the form of an Arabic translation of *Macbeth*, with some of Saddam's henchmen in bad-guy roles, or driving lessons for people who couldn't afford cars to emancipate women outside Basra was only the beginning. Here are some other actual projects that all seemed to matter at one point in time.

Pastry Class for Disadvantaged Women

"This project will provide ten classes of instruction on baking pastries and decorating cakes to twelve women who are currently unemployed," the description promised. "This small business opportunity will provide each student with skills to increase her household income, or may provide some participants with the opportunity for employment in already existing bakeries or pastry shops. A French Chef with experience in both baking pastries and in teaching pastry classes internationally will volunteer teach."[36] Who doesn't like pastry, right? And how often does a French chef pop up in a war zone? Cost: $9,797.69. (If the French chef was volunteering le time, what was the $9,797.69 spent on? Perhaps a lot of cream?) The plan was that disadvantaged Iraqi women would open cafés on bombed-out streets without water and electricity.

Artists Syndicate Play

As part of a new initiative, we paid the Iraqi Artists Syndicate to produce a play: "*Under the Donkey's Shade* focuses on an uproariously funny legal dispute that splits the people of a town into two groups. The matter in dispute is the value of shade cast by a donkey. The message is clear: Don't quarrel over minor differences. Those who see the play will get the message that political reconciliation is critical as we head into national election season. A play's just the thing to help the people focus on the importance of learning to disagree without being disagreeable."[37] A clear artsy path toward resolving Iraq's seemingly endless cycle of violence, kidnapping, terror, and sectarian strife. Cost: $22,500.

Children's Calendars

For community building and advancing civil society in rural Baghdad, publishing a calendar illustrated with Iraqi children's art would do. The Women's Association conducted an art contest for the district's children. The kiddies were given a choice of public-service themes to address (peace, neighborhood cleanliness, education, tolerance) in their art. Refreshments were served, and the twelve best works were printed on the 1,000 calendars made and distributed. The project was intended to help advance civil society and increase public awareness of common infrastructure problems.[38]

The kids who drew the pictures all got free school supplies and art materials. From their perspective, what must all this have looked like? Most of the children involved were about ten or eleven years old (hard to know as Iraqis do not typically record birthdays and so most folks knew only approximately how old they were), meaning for almost all of their sentient lives their country had always been full of American soldiers and Americans had always landed in their lives with odd things like a calendar project and their older siblings had always faced the choices of being good witches or bad witches. No one in the world had a clue whether or not, looking at the finished calendar, some kid ready to give up suddenly realized he had a future. We'd like to think so, so we did. Cost: $18,375.

Bicycles

One PRT bought 225 children's bicycles, some with training wheels, to give away as part of community development. On streets filled with trash, pockmarked with shell craters, and ruled by wild dog packs, riding the bikes was impossible. Some of the bicycle wheels were later repurposed for use on wheelchairs. Cost: $24,750.[39]

Weight-lifting Equipment

More community development, through weight lifting. Cost: $6,590.[40]

Sports Mural

A local artist was hired to paint a mural on the side of a gym—think oiled Steve Reeves musclemen. The purpose was to "provide an aesthetically pleasing sight upon entry, helping to bring a sense of normalcy for the citizens in the area and for those passing through." Cost: $22,180.[41]

Wheat Seed

Although Anbar province is mostly desert, someone on our side decided the Iraqis would grow wheat there and bought the best, most expensive seed available. The locals, knowing the crop would fail for lack of water, sold the good seed for a profit, bought some cheap stuff, and watched the sprouts die in the field. Cost of I Told You So: priceless.

Medical Gases

A large medical gases factory to create jobs and improve health care was built south of Baghdad. It failed on both counts: the owner was unable to transport the gas cylinders past Army checkpoints because terrorists used such cylinders as bomb casings. Cost: $200,000.

Internet

In areas that got maybe an hour or two of electricity each day, we filled dilapidated classrooms lacking windows, furniture, and blackboards with new computers. We then paid for a year of satellite Internet service, without a clue who would pay after our money ran out. Cost: $12,000 per school.

Baghdad Yellow Pages

In a country with few landline phones and an almost toxic environment for business, someone decided that economic success hinged on producing the first-ever Baghdad Yellow Pages. After a lot of effort, we could come up with only 250 businesses to include out of a city of several million people. My ePRT was saddled with hundreds of copies of the finished product to distribute. We could not safely go door-to-door and so hired a local contractor at seven bucks a copy to give away the books for us. Cost: $7,000.

The Baghdad Zoo

The State Department, as part of a joint effort with the Army and the USDA to revitalize the zoo, paid for computers and Internet service, ostensibly so that zoo veterinarians could use the technology to establish online relationships with vets in the United States. The thought went, if people could be shown on TV going to the zoo, it would send a message that life was returning to normal in Iraq. General Petraeus sponsored a million-dollar water park (defunct after the water pumps broke down) in Baghdad for the same reason. The zoo people revealed their collection included a large carp tattooed with an old-style Iraqi flag, the one with a Koranic verse in Saddam's own handwriting. Saddam's white horse, familiar to everyone in Iraq from hundreds of TV broadcasts, was also alive and on display. A tamed cougar kept as a pet by son Uday was available for photos. One issue the Iraqi vets needed to discuss online was whether to keep providing alcohol to the bears so they were docile toward visitors. The daily throwing of live donkeys into the lion cage at feeding time was also worthy of a Web chat. Cost: unknown.

English Language Academy for Iraqi Bureaucrats

Since Americans have such a darn hard time learning foreign languages like Arabic, why not teach the foreigners to speak

English? The Army thought it was a good idea, too, and so set aside $26 million for the Iraqi International Academy to do just that. Despite the use of an existing building that the Iraqi military kicked families out of just for us, the rehab of the place ran $13 million. The Army was pleased with the progress, and even got the British Council (the UK's official cultural arm abroad) to agree via Facebook to send a few teachers.[42] The Army forgot to involve the Iraqi government, which said it had no money to support the academy and refused to take over running the place. SIGIR intervened in early 2011 to suggest the Army not spend an additional $13 million to equip and furnish the school.[43] Cost: $13–26 million.

Road to Nowhere

After deciding a paved road would increase commerce in a particular area, the Army hired a contractor. By the time anyone checked on progress neither a paved road nor the previous rutted dirt road was there. The contractor took the money and laid down only gravel. The gravel made the road more passable, and so insurgents started to use the road as a transit route at night. The local residents appealed to the police, who set up barricades, closing off the road entirely, ending what little commerce the original dirt road had sustained. Cost: unknown.

Tarmiyah Hospital

The hospital was a major construction project. The Army finished ten rooms but did not put a roof on the facility before abandoning it for security reasons. The hospital had no power from the grid. The Iraqi Ministry of Health refused to accept the building because it did not have the staff, budget, or supply systems to open the facility—which had no roof. Cost: no one will ever know, but in the millions.

A Newspaper

When you get tired of poor media coverage, you buy your own newspaper. The Army has paid for and distributed its own newspaper, *Baghdad Now*, for years despite its having a readership of near zero. Soldiers would be tasked with handing out copies while on patrol. Costs continue to accumulate and are now in the hundreds of thousands of dollars. My ePRT paid local lawyers to write articles for the area newspaper promoting a free press without disclosing that the writers were funded by the United States. Cost: $25,000, including two generators stolen from the lawyers' offices.

There were almost too many failed projects to document, though SIGIR tried. What SIGIR called a "legacy of waste" in an August 2010 report included a $40 million prison that was never opened, a $104 million failed sewer system in Fallujah, a $171 million hospital in southern Iraq that Laura Bush "opened" in 2004 but that still has never seen a patient, and more, totaling $5 billion. Although some corruption was found, it did not account for a large amount of squandered money. Audits resulted in the restitution of only $70 million worth of embezzled funds, practically a rounding error given the $63 billion spent overall on reconstruction.[44]

Back at the old Saddam-era sports facility where we had just watched our nascent NGO training project collapse in a heap of fraud in front of our eyes, I thought about this litany of projects I had known and the money that had been spent. My thoughts were interrupted when the head of the NGO who had taken our money swept into the room and scooped us up, leading the charge out into the hallway. She took us into a room stuffed with sewing machines. Dust covered the machines and several were in pieces. The head of the NGO explained that one of my predecessors had given her $25,000 the previous year to conduct sewing classes, but unfortunately she did not have enough money to pay a teacher, so the classes were on hold. There is an Arabic expression, "A rug is never fully sold," suggesting negotiations never need end as long as one side sees money to be made. Without missing a beat, she swept her arm over the industrial waste, announced her next venture would be to teach meat processing, and asked us for another $25,000. This time we passed on the opportunity.

Promises to Keep

We not only knew the formula by now, we excelled at it. Receive LOE, create project, spend money, move on. Had we wanted to learn, we would have seen that it wasn't that hard to identify the elements of an effective project: work locally on an issue, spend money on demonstrated need, solve people's problems in a visible way. This was stuff any community organizer or humanitarian aid worker could have told us, had we set aside our hubris long enough to just ask. It was possible that the women's clinic we sponsored in Zafraniyah just might have shown us the way.

Zafraniyah was a usually violent, mixed rural and urban zone on the outskirts of Baghdad, squeezed between the Diyala and Tigris rivers. The area was now mostly Shia, with a Sunni presence. Zafraniyah was something of a case study of post-invasion Iraq, having seen a significant amount of sectarian violence after 2003 and then renewed fighting during the 2007 Surge. Its largest mosque, with a huge green dome that overlooked the main highway into town, was once Sunni. It had allegedly been taken over by the Shia Jaish al-Mahdi militia and was rumored locally to be one of their largest bases outside Sadr City. It was no surprise that in the span of ninety days there had been more than forty significant violent acts nearby.

In the midst of all this wreckage, we were approached by a local women's group looking for a way to help. What women lacked, they said, was even the most basic medical care. Facilities were sparse, and even those designed as full-spectrum medical centers failed the needs of female patients. Most women in Iraq could not see a regular doctor without the permission of a husband or father or older brother, and permission was often denied for "woman problems." It was often difficult to ensure an appointment with a female medical professional. Many hospitals and especially smaller clinics posted signs reading "Services for Men Only." We gave $84,000 to the local women's group, and the grantee opened the Al-Zafraniyah Women's Support Center.

The goal of the center was to do a small, good thing: provide a women-only option for medical care right in the community, along with creating a place where women could meet and talk about their lives. The area women were clear that they liked their veils and they liked raising their kids, and they worked hard to make sure their daughters grew up the same way. Few of our efforts acknowledged this, and many times we proceeded into failure believing the Iraqis wanted to be like us, sustained in our vision by locals who had learned that goodies would flow if they said the things we wanted to hear.

At our center, a social worker was on-site five days a week. She was available for one-on-one counseling sessions and she also met with groups of five or six women to discuss shared problems. Her meetings addressed such issues as displacement, lost and damaged property, child rearing, and the once taboo topic of domestic violence. Two lawyers on staff offered free legal advice and presented cases to local councils or courts. A legal assistant helped women collect documentation for claims and provided other administrative support as they sought to secure public assistance. The cases primarily involved obtaining social benefits from the government and the transference of pensions from deceased relatives (typically husbands killed in post-2003 violence) to the client. One woman wanted a divorce (a few years earlier, she had married a relative who had two children by his first wife; shortly after she gave birth to a daughter, the husband returned to his first wife), and another needed to legitimize her four children from an unregistered relationship, the father now dead, so that they could attend school, should schools ever reopen in the area. Another woman, fired from her job because of her political affiliation, hoped for redress from the Ministry of Industry.

A female medical doctor came to our center twice a week to see patients. She also taught first aid and led health workshops. One session covered breast cancer awareness, infections, and hygiene. The doctor began with a question-and-answer session in which some participants spoke openly for perhaps the first time about family members who were victims of breast cancer. At the end of the session, the doctor examined women by request, referred some who could afford it to hospitals, and provided limited amounts of free medicine to others.

In a typical week the doctor saw several instances of emaciation, delayed growth, and hair loss in children—all signs of malnutrition. Most of the clients were from low-income families. And because women were afraid or unable to get medical attention, small things like minor urinary infections often were not treated until they became quite serious. A typical roster:

Age 28, urinary tract infection
Age 40, untreated old tonsillitis
Age 38, kidney stone
Age 19, urinary tract infection
Age 43, arthritis
Age 43, urinary tract infection
Age 38, emaciation
Age 42, hypertension
Age 40, hypertension
Age 28, emaciation
Age 11, emaciation
Age 13, growth retardation
Age 21, delayed puberty and hair loss
Age 60, breathing difficulty
Age 60, old untreated burns affecting movement
Age 18, urinary tract infection
Age 36, lipoma in the thigh
Age 55, old untreated bone fracture

More than a hundred women and girls visited the center in its first month, though concerns about security no doubt kept many away. The project, at least, delivered on its promise, helping women in genuine need. Nevertheless, it was closed down after six months. The initial funding had run out, and US priorities had moved on to flashier economic targets. Women's centers, the Embassy announced, were not a "prudent investment."

Dairy Carey

Given the scope of the problems we confronted in Iraq, one person really could not make a big difference, though it was still possible that one person could make a small difference, and that was often worth the effort. With the slow-motion failure of our expensive milk-collection facilities on our minds, we decided that one path toward a solution lay in increasing the amount of milk farmers produced. This would give them an incentive to sell to our centers without having to abandon the existing system of selling just in the neighborhood. As luck would have it, a sister PRT was trying to get rid of someone they labeled a bit of a troublemaker, Dairy Carey. She had made up the nickname herself, having been raised plain old Carey on a dairy farm. Carey was over sixty years old, a grandma back home, and a retired employee of the US Department of Agriculture. She was rumored to not be able to stick to a plan, often balking at what she felt were dumb ideas that fell from the Green Zone and angering her team leader.

We worked with the people we could get, not the people we might have wanted in Iraq, and so, troublemaker or not, Dairy Carey was our newest ePRT team member. Despite the importance of dairy farming to the one million people in our province, we would have to make do with this single employee. She knew she could not directly reach many farmers, so Dairy Carey's plan was to train other trainers. The classes would teach them how to take better care of cows, and our new experts would then go forth and preach their knowledge. Grateful cows would in turn produce more and better milk, which the farmer could sell. Everyone would do better economically and folks would have no reason to become terrorists. We would select only female farmers as potential trainers, to secure easy funding. Eight years into the war our success now depended on cow happiness.

The problems started right as we walked in the door on the first day of class. The room was full of women, aged seventeen to about fifty-five, and only a few claimed to have ever tended to a cow. There were also lots of men milling about. While it all seemed a bit odd, a quick roll call made things worse when it turned out almost none of the "students" were the female farmers we had been told would be there. It seemed the local sheik had taken it upon himself to substitute the wives and daughters of the men in the room, all of whom were related to the sheik, in an effort to skim off a bit of the $200 salary we were going to pay those who completed the course. An attempt to generate a roster by passing around a sheet of paper demonstrated that five of the twelve students could not read or write.

Dairy Carey waded in, shooing the men out of the room and pairing each illiterate woman with one who could read and write. With the chaos sorted out, our teacher started with what seemed like some pretty commonsense tips: feed the cows better quality food and give them lots of water and you'll get more milk. Easy for us to say. For thousands of years, the handful of actual women farmers present told Dairy Carey, Iraqis had fed their cows stale bread. It was cheap to buy and bulky enough that the cows did not eat much of it. The farmers could keep feed costs low, and the bakers were happy to have a place to dump old bread. Water was a problem, too. It was hard to find and heavy to carry, and so the cows generally got water only twice a day. The cows adapted by lying around and not producing much milk. But that was all right with the people in the room, as they were not interested in getting more milk. They had no cars or trucks to transport it, no pool of employees outside the family to take on more work, and no refrigeration, and so whatever milk was produced each day was drunk at home or sold next door. Our American goal, to help Iraqis produce more milk, was irrelevant. They had a system in place that predated our idea by approximately five thousand years. More was not better.

Our agricultural grandma was undeterred. What about quality? Iraq, sadly, led the world in the transfer of tuberculosis from animals to people via unpasteurized milk. The local technique of throwing feed on the ground for the cow ensured each meal would be contaminated by the usual Jackson Pollock–like splatter of animal urine and manure. Thus Iraq also led the world in cow diseases. Some udder infections were so bad that pus came out of the teat instead of sweet creamy milk.

Ah ha! The crowd sat up. Ready to throw us out the door

for proposing to increase their milk yield, they were definitely interested in producing milk that was not deadly. Dairy Carey explained that simple tests for bacteria (similar to home pregnancy kits) could detect bad milk slightly less savagely than feeding it to babies and seeing if they lived. She gave a quick overview of germ theory, segueing smoothly into a brief history of pasteurization, followed by some slides showing basic vet tools for keeping cows healthy. In the span of minutes she had this group in rural Iraq enthralled. The rising noise level brought the men, almost all of whom were farmers, back into the room. There weren't enough chairs and from the back of the space I lost sight of Dairy Carey, surrounded now by energized men and women.

With the ice broken, the Iraqis all started talking at once about cow stomach issues. Cows eat all sorts of junk off the ground, including bits and pieces of metal that can then tear through their multiple stomachs with fatal results. Lacking the science and tech to perform surgery, the Iraqis instead forced the cow to swallow a strong magnet. The magnet attracted and held the loose metal in one part of the cow's tummy, so the cow was not shredded internally. Bovine bloat, gargantuan gas, was a huge issue. Without access to medication, the farmers poured soda down the cow's throat, which made the cows belch in a horrific way but cured the bloat. While missing some steps in modern science like germ theory and pasteurization, the locals had nailed large portions of folk medicine. One exception: some problems were still resolved by tying a written prayer from the imam onto the cow's tail. Dairy Carey stood on a chair to direct the conversation, acknowledging the folk cures while explaining what the modern vet tools and limited medicines we could provide would do to help make better milk. Quantity was thrown out in favor of quality, a first for our ePRT, maybe for any PRT.

Dairy Carey did indeed make some waves, sometimes even getting a little wet, but in our case she jettisoned a well-written plan that would have failed anyway to give people something they needed, something they could see would help. In Iraq, we were faced regularly with such frustrations and such cynicism that when something, anything, seemed to work, it was a special day.

4-H Club Comes to Iraq

When we tried to grow oaks from acorns overnight, it didn't work. But our agriculture team's modest attempt to set up a 4-H club in Mahmudiyah set down tender, delicious roots, Dairy Carey at work again. 4-H is a well-known agricultural club for kids, a kind of Boy Scouts for little farmers. In the United States, 4-H (the four *H*s stand for head, heart, hands, and health) teaches farm things, like how to raise animals, and also citizenship, manners, getting along—that kind of stuff. Even though 4-H was new to Iraq, approximately twenty-four children showed up. The children introduced themselves and we had a short discussion about the donated computers (old laptops from our office scheduled for the trash, or more likely the black market by way of the trash). We talked about the election of officers, the upcoming pen pal program with a 4-H club in Montana, and the care of lambs donated to the club by a well-to-do local farmer. The club would teach the kids how to raise the lambs.

"Design a Clover," as the 4-H symbol is a four-leaf clover, was the last activity. The kids wrote out their goals, one on each leaf. Most of them wanted to learn how to use computers and a few hoped to play better soccer or learn to swim. One veiled twelve-year-old girl was crying, so we pulled her aside to see what the problem was. Her parents had never sent her to school; in Iraq's male-dominated society only her brother had received an education. She could not read or write and thus, of course, could not write a goal on her paper clover. We helped her laboriously write out "I want to read" and invited her back. We'd try to teach her to read a little.

Nothing breeds incest among PRTs better than success, and buoyed by our photos of the kids, other PRTs started their own 4-H clubs. Our club idea even threatened to dethrone widows from their position atop the PRT project ziggurat. Unfortunately, our success also attracted attention at the Embassy, feeding its desire for some media.

Real good news was hard to find, so when it happened we tended to overdo it. Even worse was when we manufactured the illusion of good news and beat the hell out of that. Look at the story of Operation Little Yasser. A sister PRT singled out an orphan and built a whole phony project around him, something about bringing a greenhouse to an orphanage so the kids could heal by growing squash. The kid, Yasser, was just a prop for the media to write stories about, describing him as a "sweet, fragile child, whose soulful eyes reveal some of the heartbreak he's endured." The kid did not get anything out of his exploitation, kids rarely do, but the Embassy sure got some major PR miles. Who knows if the orphanage ever got the greenhouse?

For our 4-H club, the Embassy lined up several local reporters paid by—er, supportive of—the United States for the trip out to our kids. Because the room we used for meetings was singularly unphotogenic, we had to cajole a local sheik with promises of a new well to open his house for us. The guy rose to the challenge, throwing in for the cameras both an impassioned defense of the American invasion and a strong push for a well on his property. The Embassy handlers' request for shots of kids together with their animals failed when one of the critters, left roped to a pole in the sun too long, passed out. Nonetheless, the kids made some cute remarks on camera, and a *Washington Post* stringer later picked up the story. I, too, was interviewed, having first been reminded by the Embassy team to give most of the credit to my boss. At least everyone was excited to see themselves on TV that night.

We had once again stumbled blindly onto a winning formula. The Iraqi parents who sat in on our first sessions took control of the club, without our paying them to do it. They organized a visit to a local dentist's office and all the kids got free cleanings, the first dental care many had ever received. Eager to help further, the dentist scheduled appointments for a few kids with obvious cavities before enrolling his own children in 4-H. Not to be outdone, the farmer who donated the lambs now wanted to donate other animals for the kids to raise. The adults organized a trip to a local civic hall, where another group we had not paid displayed their paintings. Civic leaders who wanted in on the club bought hats for the kids.

After almost a year in Iraq for this ePRT, the 4-H club was still our most successful project, maybe our only genuinely successful one. We spent almost no money on it, empowered no local thugs, did not distort the local economy, turned it over as soon as possible to the local Iraqis, and got out of the way. The kids' selection of officers for the club was their first experience of grassroots democracy. The powerful sheik's son went home crying because he lost the race for the presidency to a farmer's kid, and the sheik did not have anyone's throat slit in retaliation. The things the club had to look forward to, pen pals in Montana and more animals, were real and could be done without any money from outside. There remained the tiniest possibility here, where in most everything else we had done there was none, that a year later there would still be a 4-H club in Iraq.

The morning after one meeting, an IED detonated at the Mahmudiyah local government building, just across the street from where the 4-H club met. The city council chairperson was slightly injured, along with two others. The explosion happened within eyesight of the building guards, who saw nothing, of course. None of the 4-H kids were around, but we all thought the same thing: twenty-four hours earlier, what would have happened?

This was what tore you apart in Iraq, that every small step forward seemed followed by some tragedy. If I were religious I would have asked why God fucked with these people, and if I was me I would try to believe the sum of karma, the weight of good on one side and bad on the other, would someday, somehow balance, even though I could not for the life of me imagine what that process would be. Much as we tried to stick a finger in the dike to block the cynicism that otherwise washed over us, we ended up most nights drinking hard, cursing the darkness.

Checkpoints

A SIGACT is milspeak for a "significant action." Some things were always significant, such as the death of a soldier, while other things, like destruction of a campaign poster, might be significant in the run-up to an election and not important at all a month later. The bases kept logs of SIGACTs and, following whatever criteria their boss set, soldiers would add things to the log as required. Often the log was updated right from the field via a satellite communications system called Blue Force Tracker. Given the combination of a lame on-screen keyboard and a Vehicle Commander typing in a moving truck, these SIGACT entries were often terse, full of acronyms, quickly classified under a default setting, and then forgotten. The locations were usually expressed in the form of a grid, a series of numbers that referred to classified maps. The more numbers, the more specific the location (8734961230 was a place your

friend died). You needed an interpreter to read a SIGACT
entry.

AT 2036, (——) WAS ATTACKED BY IDF IVO BALAD. RADAR
ACQUIRED THE POO VIC (——) CONDUCTED CF WITH
6×155MM HE. NO INJ/DAMAGE.

Translation: At 8:36 at night, location (——) was hit by
indirect fire from the vicinity of Balad, a nearby town. Our
radar located the point of origin in the vicinity of (——). We
fired back with six shots of 155mm high-explosive artillery.
There were no injuries or damage on our side.

One category stood out from the mountain of SIGACT
reports: AIF attacks on CPs, or anti-Iraqi forces attacks on a
checkpoint. The idea of checkpoints was that by stopping
vehicles, well, everywhere, all the time, soldiers, cops, Sons of
Iraq, militiamen, and anyone else with a gun had a chance to
prevent the easy flow of weapons, bad guys, and car bombs. You
couldn't drive very far anywhere in urban Iraq without stopping
at a checkpoint to have your ID looked at and your vehicle
searched. Checkpoint duty was so ubiquitous at one point in the
war that even *Doonesbury* spoofed it.[45] Some searches were
thorough, some lazy, and bribery at Iraqi-manned checkpoints
was a regular option for those with something to hide as well as
those in a legitimate hurry.

By 2009, the United States was no longer responsible for
most checkpoints in Iraq, though we regularly sent our guys
out to "advise and assist" the Iraqis. I spent a sweaty cold night
at a checkpoint on the outskirts of Baghdad hanging around
with soldiers who spent more than too many nights out there.
Soldiers who would joke about anything—a dead dog, your

divorce, child porn—became really quiet on a 'point. Within the limits of available electricity, they would try to light up the spot as best they could (you could run only so many watts if all you had was some crappy Chinese portable generator) so drivers could see them. Iraq at night was a dark and dangerous place, and drivers were not going to slow down or, God forbid, stop without a good reason. So step one was to brighten up your checkpoint so the drivers couldn't miss it. The next step was to somehow communicate to drivers that they had to stop. There was no such thing as getting a license in Iraq; someone showed you how to drive and that was it. Driving a truck was sought-after employment, so fibbing about actually knowing how to drive was popular. It was possible the guy heading toward your checkpoint had never passed one before.

Standing at a checkpoint in a dense area was easier than out in the countryside, as the jammed-up traffic meant cars approached at a crawl and everyone had time to signal their intentions across cultures and languages. In the suburbs or on a lesser-traveled road, things got stickier. You could start with big signs in Arabic and English that told folks to slow down, but there was that light problem again, plus many Iraqis were illiterate. You could set up all manner of flashers and twirling things—a good start but ambiguous. Drivers might think it was a wedding party (plenty of guns there as well).

Car bombs were a big thing to be scared of at a checkpoint. Usually the explosives were intended for some other target and were just passing through your 'point. But if the driver thought you were on to him, he'd blow up the car bomb right there and never mind the real target. Checkpoints also made everyone nervous, and nervous people and guns were a bad mix. Iraqi drivers hit the gas a lot, worried, angry, maybe feeling the need to show the US Army who had the big brass ones in a really dumb way.

As cars approached, soldiers would be thinking about the ROE, rules of engagement, which stipulate when you are allowed to kill someone legally. Even wars have rules, and nobody went outside the wire without knowing exactly what they were. ROEs changed all the time, but at a checkpoint they typically went like this: Try to stop the car with lights, sound, and hand gestures. If it keeps coming, try shining a laser or bright light at the driver (called "beaming"). If that does not work, fire a warning shot or a nonlethal round. Still coming? Fire into the engine block to disable the car. Not enough? Kill the driver.

In theory, this all seemed logical enough. In reality, it didn't work as well. The soldier might have been up the last eighteen hours on patrol and is staying awake only with the constant application of Rip It energy drinks and instant coffee crystals crunched between bites of candy. Last night one of his buddies was almost killed by a driver who got scared and hit the gas. He is on the move and sweating despite the cool weather because standing still anywhere, never mind under bright lights, can attract snipers and he does not want to get popped. The vehicle approaching has only one headlight and it looks like there are several people in the front seat, where there are usually only one or two. In the span of three seconds he needs to try to wave down the driver, beam him with the laser if the guy doesn't slow down, fire a nonlethal round if he keeps going, and then switch weapons and be ready to take a life. He's Zeus, fucking Thor throwing lightning bolts. Make the decision. Shoot or don't shoot the motherfucker. Decide, asshole.

He doesn't shoot this time. He gets to decide many times every night.

The vehicle with one headlight slowed down of its own accord late in the cycle. Maybe the driver couldn't find the brake, maybe the brake didn't work, maybe he was rehearsing for a suicide run later that week, who knows, he slowed and stopped. Front seat full of kids, driver dad, mom in the backseat with a baby. They stopped, the search came up empty, the IDs didn't have any of the unpronounceable Iraqi names on the bad-guy list. The hard stares from the passengers said "fuck you" without a word's being passed. They pulled out, maybe eyeing the weapon but likely with no idea the soldier had just weighed their lives against his. He chugged another hit of energy drink and waited for the next car. No SIGACT. It could take a lot of balls to not shoot someone at a checkpoint. Some nights things went well, and some nights he went back to the FOB knowing why this shit sucked so much.

1045 ON IVO BALAD ROUTE (——): (——) CIV WIA (——) CIV KIA AIF ATTACKED THE ENTRANCE TO CP. (——) AND (——) (CHILD—(——) WERE KILLED AND 6X WIA.

Translation: At 10:45 in the morning in the vicinity of Balad, on Route (——), near the town of Balad, there were civilians wounded in action and civilians killed in action after anti-Iraq forces attacked the entrance to a checkpoint. (——) and (——) plus a child named (——) were killed and six others were wounded.

Seeing the Dragon

BANG! Just like that.

Being mortared was like a sneeze coming on; you knew it was going to happen but there was nothing you could do about it. The insurgents' targeting was never precise, more like "somewhere on the FOB," and your job was to not be standing on the invisible X when the rounds hit. Maybe roulette was a better example; one of those numbers was going to win (lose), but there was no way to tell. Pay your money, take your chance.

The worst mortar attack on FOB Falcon ripped apart a containerized housing unit, leaving torn shards of metal poking out of the sides like ugly silver flowers. I was outside when it happened. First there was a little boom when the mortar was shot off and then a second later a big boom hit my chest like a fist. People died. Another time a bomb went off right next to my wall while I was in the shower. The blast was all on the outside but the shock wave was strong enough to make me lose my balance. In the space of six months, the insurgents mortared or rocketed FOB Falcon over seventy times, meaning you had to get used to not being used to it—my luck was tested more than my courage. Even with a lot of practice I couldn't manage to pretend my body and the cheap trailer I lived in were not fragile as a biscuit.

This was what we came to call passive violence—you stood there and it happened to you, like weather—but it was still whack dangerous. There was no warning for these kinds of attacks, and of course you never knew who was firing on you. The insurgents had learned to keep the trajectory of their mortars flat to avoid our shell-seeking radar. One minute I would be getting up from dinner and the next a shell would strike in front of me. It would happen too quickly for me to be scared; instead I would be scared for the next time. While there was no warning, there was usually no aftereffect either. The shell hit, a big plume of dust went up, and then the breeze blew the dust away. Gun shots were just as disconcerting. The first time I got shot at there was a zipping sound in the air, like a nasty insect passing that was small and big at the same time. I never saw the person who fired at me and I never had a moment to react, human reaction time and bullet physics being what they are. I stood there like an idiot asking, "What was that?" while the soldier with me smiled like I was six years old, the dumbest son of a bitch he had ever seen.

What would we do if we came under fire? This was the question we chewed over endlessly. Raised on war movies and video games, many of us wanted to see it and feel it and to go home knowing we'd been tested. A Major who was too old too young overheard these conversations and told us we were stupid. He said people who got shot at got hurt, and once you saw someone hurt you carried that around with you. You'd wrestle those images for freaking ever. As the Chinese saying goes, you can't unsee the dragon. Once you've seen it, it's always with you.

Modern weapons were designed to destroy human beings with maniacal efficiency, to shred and tear flesh and shatter, not break, bones. In real life, things are built specifically to prevent harm. My lawn mower has all sorts of guards and safety switches and at home we round off sharp edges and take slippery rugs off the stairs. I was shocked when I held a mortar shell for the first time—it was deliberately designed to cause the worst possible injuries, with grooves cut into the exterior so it would break apart easily and split into shards. Smart people had gone out of their way to make this thing as deadly as they could.

Soldiers took the necessary precautions. They wrote their blood type on their boots on the theory that, unless your leg was blown off, your boots would stay on. I heard about a "meat tattoo" where soldiers had their blood type, name, and social security number tattooed on their torso somewhere so they could be identified. Despite these steps, standard medical help in the so-called golden hour following a trauma was no longer enough. As weapons had become more lethal, the golden hour was now compressed to minutes. The only way any of us would survive a catastrophic injury was if the guy next to us did exactly the right thing right now. The Army called it "be quick or be dead."

So each of us was a medic and we each carried a pouch with a tourniquet, a bandage, and some blood-clotting agent. If you got hurt, someone grabbed the stuff from your pouch and took care of you. In eighth-grade first aid, we learned that a tourniquet was a last, desperate measure because of the risk it might cut off so much blood flow that you'd lose a limb. In this war, the rule was tourniquet first. Some guys even pulled the tourniquet out of the pouch before going out and had it hanging off their vest for double-quick use. Those extra seconds could mean the difference between living or dying or losing a limb—that, and how well the person with you had done his training. The Army tried to teach soldiers What to Do in every circumstance that could be anticipated, to pound the right lessons into even the dumbest recruit. One of the more extreme things they did to simulate injuries and practice lifesaving before deploying was to work on live tissue.

The preferred victim was an anesthetized pig. The new recruit was given a pig and he had to keep it alive. "Every time I did something to help him," one soldier told an interviewer, "they would wound him again. They shot him twice in the face with a 9mm pistol and then six times with an AK-47 and then twice with a 12-gauge shotgun. And then he was set on fire. I kept him alive for 15 hours."[46]

The guys at Falcon who had been selected for the training all started with a big 180-pound, man-sized hog. The trainers blew half the pig's face away, slit open its belly, and cut the femoral artery. The idea was to get the soldiers to ignore the horrific facial wound and the slit belly and focus on the femoral. If you couldn't stop it from pushing blood out, your pig/soldier/friend bled to death in minutes. The soldiers topped one another with ghastly descriptions of how messed up their pigs had been. The trainers were never done. As soon as you controlled one thing, they shot, cut, or tore the pig in another way. At one point they threw the bleeding pig into the back of a pickup truck and you had to continue to work to save its life as the truck bounced down a rutted back road in North Carolina. The session ended with everyone covered in blood and the pig ultimately mutilated. Anesthetized or not, it was a crappy way to die. Animal rights groups often protested this type of training, and the Army was forced to conduct it in semisecrecy. Soldiers who had undergone the experience were careful when and how they talked about it. No one enjoyed seeing an animal suffer, and most left the sessions with questions in their heads about right and wrong. What was a pig's life worth?

On Route Incubus, outside Falcon, an EFP struck the vehicle a Lieutenant and his Sergeant were riding in. An EFP is an explosively formed penetrator, a steel cylinder about the size and shape of a big paint can filled with explosives. Instead of a lid, the can was sealed with a milled copper plate, a kind of metal lens with a concave bottom. When the explosives detonated, the copper lens turned into a white-hot liquid slug, propelled at enormous speed.

The slug melted through the armor and met the upper side of the Lieutenant's right thigh, about halfway between his unarmored knee and his unarmored hip. The slug, still hot, melted the skin and muscle of the Lieutenant's leg. His femur was solid, like a young man's dense bones are, but the slug shattered the bone by force. No one was sure if it was the slug or bone fragments, but something sliced through the femoral artery and at that moment, as the slug cooled and ultimately came to rest against the metal interior of the vehicle, the Lieutenant, at age twenty-seven, began the short process of bleeding to death.

The copper slug did not hit the Sergeant seated across from the Lieutenant, but his face was peppered with metal fragments and his upper body was covered with the remains of his Lieutenant's thigh. Surfing his own pain, he acted immediately, without thinking. When the Army decorated him for saving his friend's life, the Sergeant said he had imagined him as a pig. He remembered applying a tourniquet to a pig's leg, remembered clamping off a pig's femoral artery, and remembered how he had worked with a pig's ripped flesh and shattered bone all over his face. When called to do exactly the right thing, the Sergeant answered correctly, and that made the difference. There were a lot of ways to die in Iraq and only a few ways to keep on living.

Missing Him

Private First Class (PFC) Brian Edward Hutson, in Iraq, put the barrel of his M-4 semiautomatic assault rifle into his mouth, with the weapon set for a three-round burst, and blew out the back of his skull. He was college-aged but had not gone and would never go to college. Notice appeared in the newspapers a week after his death, listed as "non-combat-related."

Of the 4,471 American military deaths in Iraq, 913 were considered "non-combat-related," that is, nonaccidents, suicides. In 2010, as in 2009, more soldiers died by their own hand than in combat.[47] Perhaps related, mental disorders in those years outpaced injuries as a cause for hospitalization. The Army reported a record number of suicides in a single month for June 2010. Thirty-two soldiers in all, more than one a day for the whole month.[48] Given that suicides sometimes occurred after soldiers departed Iraq, and given that death by enemy action was no longer as common, their lives were probably in as much danger at home as in Iraq.

The M-4 rifle PFC Hutson used to kill himself, successor to the M-16 of Vietnam fame, allows the shooter, with the flip of a switch, to choose to fire one bullet per trigger pull or three. Nobody knows whether PFC Hutson spent a long time or no time with the rifle barrel in his mouth, but he must have really wanted to be dead, because he chose three shots. The bullets exploded through his brain in sequence. He left his toilet kit in the shower trailer. He still had Clearasil in the bag. Rumor was he'd had trouble sleeping.

I heard about his death at breakfast and walked over to his trailer. I took a quick look inside and saw the fan spray of blood and brain on the wall, already being washed off by the Bangladeshi cleaning crew. The bleach solution they used was smearing more than cleaning, and the Bangladeshis had little stomach to wring out the mop heads all that often. Blood like this smelled coppery. It reminded you that you were not welcome. Even if you'd never smelled pooled blood before, you didn't have to learn what it was, you already knew something was wrong in this place.

Death does not redeem or disgrace. It is just a mess and no one who deals with it thinks otherwise. Don't ask poets or pastors, because they do not know that pieces of people still look a lot like people and that extreme violence leaves bodies looking nothing like the bodies you see in open caskets or on TV. In Iraq I saw a girl crushed when a wall collapsed, her face looking like a Halloween pumpkin a few days too late. There was a drowned man in an irrigation ditch, gray and bloated, no eyes, no fucking eyes. Fish had nibbled them.

A week before Hutson's suicide, another soldier lost his life. This soldier, a turret gunner, was killed when his vehicle unsuccessfully tried to pass at thirty-five miles per hour under a too-low bridge. The Army counted deaths by accident as "combat deaths," while suicides were not. Under a policy followed by George W. Bush and for more than two years by Barack Obama, the families of suicides do not receive a condolence letter from the President. Suicides apparently do not pertain to freedom. They died *of* the war, but not *in* the war.

But if distinctions between causes of death were made at the Pentagon, that was not the case on the ground in Iraq. The death of any soldier reverberated through the FOB. This was, after all, a small town, and nobody was left untouched. The comfort of ritual stood in for public expressions of actual feelings, which were best kept private and close. And the ritual prescribed by regulation was the same, whether the death was by suicide or in combat. The chapel had rows of chairs set up, much as it would in Hamilton, Ohio, or Marietta, Georgia, for a wedding, only at the front of the room was a wooden box, made and brought to Iraq for this purpose, with holes for the US and the unit flag and a slot to stand the deceased's rifle. The remains of the deceased were likely already on their way home and not with us. The box was made of plywood, stained and varnished like paneling, and reminded everyone of a B+ wood shop project. The dead man's boots stood on either side of the rifle, with his helmet on top. It was fitting no one had cleaned the boots, because the presence of the dust and dirt wiped away a lot of the cheapness of the ritual. Before the event started, the hum in the room was about future meetings, upcoming operations, food in the chow hall, the workaday talk of soldiers.

There was a program, done up on a word processor, with the official Army photo of the deceased, wearing a clean uniform, posed in front of an American flag—young, so young, you could see a few red pockmarks on the side of his face, a chicken pox scar on his forehead. All these photos showed a vacant stare, same as every high school graduation photo. The program was standard fare—some speeches, the chaplain reading the 23rd Psalm, and a final good-bye.

The speeches were strained because the senior officers who feel it important to speak at these events rarely knew, or could know among the many troops under them, the deceased. As with every other briefing they gave, albeit without the Power-Point, the officers read words someone else wrote for them to give the impression of authority and familiarity. The dead man's job had something minor to do with radios and most present couldn't say much beyond that. The eulogy thus rang a bit hollow, but you reminded yourself that the words were not necessarily intended for you and that the Colonel may not have been the best man for the job. He was a responsible man, trying hard to do something impossible, and he probably felt bad for his lack of conviction. He did understand why we were all here, and that a task had to be done, and that he need not be Pericles or Lincoln to do a decent job of it.

The last speaker was by tradition someone acquainted personally with the deceased, a friend if one could be found, a junior leader or coworker if not. In today's ceremony, things were especially awkward. The dead man had taken his life and had done so after only a few months in the Army and even less time at this FOB. Nobody really had befriended him, and this being the third suicide on the FOB made the whole thing especially grim. The ceremony felt rushed, like an overrehearsed school play where the best performance had taken place the night before.

But sometimes things surprised you, maybe because of low expectations, maybe because every once in a while somebody stood up and said just what needed to be said. A young Captain rose without notes. "I was his team leader but I never really knew him. Brian was new here. He didn't have no nickname and he didn't spend much time with us. He played Xbox a lot. We don't know why he committed suicide. We miss him anyway because he was one of us. That's all I have to say."

This was how the Army healed itself. It was a simple organization, a vast group of disparate people who came together for their own reasons, lived in austere conditions, and existed to commit violence under bewildering circumstances. Simply, we will miss him anyway because he was one of us. The word that raised the sentence beyond simple declaration was "anyway." It was important to believe we all meant something to one another because we were part of this. When it rained, we all got wet. We could hate the war, hate the President, hate the Iraqis, but we could not hate one another.

The ceremony ended with the senior enlisted person calling the roll for the dead man's unit. Each member answered, "Here, Sergeant Major" after his name was called. That was until the name called was the dead man's. "Brian Hutson?" Silence. "Brian E. Hutson?" Silence. "Private First Class Brian Edward Hutson?" Silence. Brian was not there and almost none of us had known him but yes, today, at this place, we all missed him anyway.

What Victory Looks Like

On a rare cloudy day, we drove Aida, an ePRT Iraqi employee, through a twisty maze of S-curves, barricades, and checkpoints toward the edge of the base. It was her last day with the team and an American supervisor needed to follow her to the exit to take possession of her ID card so she could never reenter Falcon.

Aida was one of the better people we had hired. Before the invasion, she was a professor of English at a major Baghdad university. She had a PhD and around the office people jokingly called her "doctor," though she never laughed along. Because she had had to join Saddam's Baath party at age twenty-seven to get her teaching job, she had been thrown out of work by the Americans in 2003 as part of the crude de-Baathification process that swept up everyone from Chemical Ali to preschool teachers. Several years later things changed, and such nonsubstantive party membership as our employee once held was understood to be nonsubstantive. By then, however, the insurgency had started, the universities were closed, and there were no jobs for professors. With what I wanted to hope was some sense of irony, Aida started working for the Army, as a 'terp, what the Army insists on calling interpreters. Her English was near fluent and she even understood the soldiers' dark humor, but the work did not challenge her and she was bored. For her own protection we paid her in cash, forty dollars a day, so there was no paper trail to show she worked for us. Aida, of course, was not her real name, as she hid her actual identity even from a bunch of Americans unlikely to ever be able to pronounce it correctly.

The little anteroom we used for out-processing at the gate was separated from Earth. A bit bigger than my parents' downstairs closet, it had no air-conditioning and no ventilation. The air did not move. Time did not move. Every surface was covered in the gray tan dust of Iraq. A Ugandan guard stood with a machine gun in one corner, watching us. Another Ugandan stood behind a dusty counter window and stuck his hand out wordlessly for Aida's base pass. He returned her cell phone from the rack; the rules prohibited local employees from having cell phones on the FOB so they could not call to confederates or trigger bombs remotely. The Ugandan guard then called a female Ugandan, presumably not to offend Muslim sensibilities, to search the three plastic shopping bags our employee had with her. The female guard pulled items of clothing out of the bags, looking at each piece as if weighing it as a purchase. The search took a long time, and the Ugandan kept making eye contact with me, as if hoping I would object so she would have an excuse to slow down even further. But I knew the game and I ignored her, and she had no reason to give me any guff.

The inspection complete, Aida was told to walk out the door, which led to a narrow dog run about fifty yards long, fenced on both sides with razor wire. This was the regular way on and off the FOB. She had explained to us that because working for the Americans endangered her and her family, and because she was sure the gate was almost certainly watched, she always took a taxi into central Baghdad, got out at some random crowded place, and then, after walking around a bit, hopped into a second cab to go home. The idea was to obscure any direct line between us and the life she led outside the FOB. As she walked away between the razor wire, I thanked Aida for her work and called good-bye. She did not answer and did not look back. Maybe she did not hear me, though I spoke plain and loud enough.

It was then very quiet, one of those odd punctuation moments when the traffic noise stops suddenly and you have a chance to snatch at the thoughts in your head. Following what we intended to be the liberation of her country, Aida had lost her profession and her livelihood, had found her life endangered by the only work she could come up with, and had received a meager, short-term handout from us that improved her prospects not at all. When our needs changed, we took even that away and walked her to the exit.

So how did we end up accomplishing so little when we meant well? On the ground, at my ePRT level, ego played a role, as team leaders liked saying yes to their bosses, liked being "befriended" by locals, liked to brag about how connected they were to their assigned area communities by virtue of building and bankrolling stuff. This was the game we were required to play. Visitors from the Embassy demanded to meet "real" Iraqis, but only under safe conditions, and preferably ones who spoke English and would pose for photos in robes and who could be summoned on short notice, even on holidays and Friday prayer days, to accommodate the visitors' inflexible schedules. We were all required to have a few such Iraqi friends to keep our bosses happy, and friends didn't come for free.

The physical reality, that we lived imprisoned on military bases, meant that we had the most cursory relationships with Iraqis and were always seen as fat-walleted aliens descending from armored spaceships. The professionals and the technocrats, the doctors and engineers who might have been partners in reconstruction, had fled to other countries (20,000 of Iraq's 34,000 registered physicians had chosen exile).[49] We were left to spend our money among thugs, thieves, tribal leaders with self-serving agendas, and corrupt government officials placed in their jobs by the United States.

Our attention spans were short and our desire to examine the results was limited. The terms *Iraqi good* or *good enough for Iraq* stood in for any substantive quality checks. Soldiers would joke about "drive-by QA/QC," where a quick run past some project would replace serious quality assurance or quality check inspection. The same sloppiness applied to staffing. If a guy had been assistant night manager at a KFC back home, he was made a small business adviser in Iraq. A Sergeant who fixed cars ended up overseeing a vocational school. We made desperate use of hobbies and tangential skills in lieu of real project management. The contractors took advantage of our sloppiness, and the Iraqis we were supposed to help got junk from us.

Many good intentions floundered as personnel departed Iraq. Most people stayed no longer than twelve months, and they usually believed history began when they first stepped onto Iraqi soil. Our memory barely extended back beyond a few months. The child rape-murder atrocity committed by American soldiers and chronicled in Jim Frederick's book *Black Hearts: One Platoon's Descent into Madness in Iraq's Triangle of Death* took place in our area of responsibility a little before my time, yet no one in all my preparatory briefings ever mentioned it. They might not have known about it themselves but I'm pretty sure the Iraqis I worked with remembered. The Iraqis were here for the last group and here for this one. We have the watch, but they have the time, says an old joke.

Our short-term memory should come as no surprise, sent to war as we were by people who failed to understand that history started a long time ago. As Andrew Bacevich observes in *Washington Rules: America's Path to Permanent War*, when an event like Saddam's invasion of Kuwait in 1990 or the terrorist attacks of 9/11 "disrupts the American pursuit of peace, . . . those exercising power in Washington invariably depict the problem as appearing out of the blue, utterly devoid of historical context. The United States is either the victim or an innocent bystander, Washington's own past actions possessing no relevance to the matter at hand."[50]

We lacked not only history but guidance. At all levels there was little direction to relate what we did at the ePRT to the broader goals we heard at the Embassy, such as the creation of a democratic Iraq or defeating the terrorists. We had to make it up on our own. Every ePRT went through fads and fashions in its year, holding women's empowerment conferences, paying for trash pickup, or giving away books and school supplies. The local community often served as the only record of what had previously been proposed, promised, or done. Most ePRT and military leaders walked into first meetings with local power brokers to learn of projects we were supposedly committed to undertake. Though often suspecting we were being swindled, we actually welcomed their claims as a way of providing us with some direction.

A variety of systems were created to track things, and every ePRT produced a "maturity model" matrix, layers of work plans, progress modeling reports, mission statements, strategic goals, charts of lines of effort, and the like. Owing to their length, complexity, and untethered-to-reality focus, these reporting tools were useless for planning and quickly devolved into a list of chores to be done, like cleaning the garage. Within my own year in Iraq, we switched progress models repeatedly, the changes making it impossible to compare progress from year to year, possibly the unspoken point of it all. Reporting obsessively on our "greatest accomplishments and greatest challenges" forced us to exaggerate or create something new to say every few days. If we didn't do it, our bosses editing our reports would. No Embassy leader ever got (or wanted) an accurate report.

Under a system where we proceeded without much direction or assessment, we could not win, but we could lose if something we tried offended someone in the Embassy. Given the long-term scale for progress in development and counterinsurgency, the best thing for people on a one-year tour was to take no chances, do as asked, and stay below the radar. This was what led to the preponderance of widow projects, for example, because they were safe. Reports to the head office often brought a rebuke for some initiative that crossed a line you never knew existed in the ever-skittish Embassy political section. Working with one eye on Iraq and one on the Embassy was difficult. I never once had a project I approved substantively questioned at any level, but all hell broke loose when I canceled two. The safest bet was to give in to the kindergarten system, which judged performance by effort rather than results. Activity was valued over insight.

A military colleague working with another ePRT summed it all up, saying, "State is less concerned about what actually gets done. They don't establish metrics for themselves, or measure accomplishments. More interested in process, policy, effective communication and establishing connections that allow them to generate good reports. The frustration with the State Department is that they are very happy just to be. And whether or not anything actually gets done is not important to them."[51]

Robert Kaplan, in the *Atlantic*, saw the PRTs as "smoke and mirrors operations. . . . As a concept, they have been successfully sold to the outside world, but they have yet to be sufficiently staffed and bureaucratically developed. They provide useful fodder for pep talks to the media, but on the ground, they run the risk of irrelevance."[52]

The deputy head of the Office of the Special Inspector General for Iraq Reconstruction offered a more charitable assessment of PRTs: "There's a difference between 'could we have done better?' and 'did we do nothing at all?' I think it's somewhere in between."[53]

The thing most folks said about the PRTs' work was that it was ignorant (yes) and wasteful (yes, but by small amounts when the overall war cost $1 billion a week) but that really, at the end of the day, what was the harm? If a woman learned to drive, someone enjoyed a play, or a widow baked some wonderful date tarts, what was the harm?

The harm was this: We wanted to leave Iraq stable and independent, with the strength to resist insurgency. But how did we advance that goal when we spent our time and money on obviously pointless things, while most people lacked access to clean water, or regular electricity, or schools and hospitals. How did we help stabilize Iraq when we acted like buffoons? Spending money on plays and beekeeping kits must have seemed like insanity, or stupidity, or corruption, or all three. As one Iraqi said, "It is like I am standing naked in a room with a big hat on my head. Everyone comes in and helps put flowers and ribbons on my hat, but no one seems to notice that I am naked." An ePRT team leader wrote in his weekly summary, "At our project ribbon-cuttings we are typically greeted now with a cursory 'thank you,' followed by a long list of crushing needs for essential services such as water and power."

We grasped that military action could take us only so far, but we failed to understand the next stage. Historian Bernard Fall, writing in 1965 about our efforts in Vietnam, said that counterinsurgency wars are won "not through military action . . . but through an extremely well-conceived civic action program and, of course, a good leader. . . . Civic action is not the construction of privies or the distribution of antimalaria sprays. One can't fight an ideology; one can't fight a militant doctrine with better privies."[54] Another writer, blogging haiku-style in 2010 about Afghanistan, expressed the idea even more succinctly:

> Effective Leaders
> Control the Population
> Allow us to leave[55]

As both writers noted, a key element in counterinsurgency is establishing a local government that can stand on its own because the people believe in their leaders. Field Manual 3-24, General Petraeus's best-selling doctrine for counterinsurgency operations, argued, "The primary objective of any counterinsurgency operation is to foster development of effective governance by a legitimate government."[56] In Iraq, we never held local elections and never pressured the Iraqis to hold them. At a national level, Iraq went most of a year after the March 2010 elections with no one in charge.

Corruption was endemic. In 2010, a Baghdad newspaper reported the salaries of key government people. The highest paid was Jalal Talabani, who the paper claimed made close to $700,000 a year. The Prime Minister, his boss, pulled in $360,000, and two underlings made $170,000 each. The salaries were a small part of overall compensation, with allowances of $15,000 a month for transportation and $30,000 for entertainment.[57] Members of Parliament made $129,000 a year, with similar allowances and a hefty 80 percent pension for life waiting for them after only four years of service.[58] Meanwhile, 25 percent of Iraqis lived below the poverty line, set at $60 a month.[59] The United Nations in 2009 estimated 57 percent of all Iraqis lived in slums. In the worst areas, such as Maysan and Diyala, over 80 percent lived in slums. Pre-2003, the average number of slum dwellers was 20 percent.[60]

We controlled the moment the war started, but we couldn't control when it ended except by walking away. After years of seeking a military solution, followed by years of building ineffective privies through our ePRTs, we simply declared victory and started to pack up. As one sheik told me, "You dug a deep hole in 2003 and now are walking away leaving it empty." America sneezed and Iraq caught the cold.

We meant well, most of us really did. Hubris stalked us; we suffered from arrogance and we embraced ignorance. Hew Francis Anthony Strachan, in volume 1 of his *First World War*, wrote, "Courage takes two forms in war. Courage in the face of personal danger, a requirement for tactical success . . . and courage to take responsibility, a requirement for strategic success." In our reconstruction efforts there was no question about our courage in the face of personal danger, but we lacked the courage to be responsible. It was almost as if a new word were needed, *disresponsible*, a step beyond irresponsible, meaning you should have been the one to take responsibility but shucked it off.

At the end of my tour, I still had forty-six calendars made by Iraqi kids in a dusty pile in my office. The media blitz over for that project, no one wanted them. We left the calendars behind when we closed the office and moved on.

Exhaling: Leaving Iraq

"Tell me how this ends," General David Petraeus famously asked a reporter during the early days of the Iraqi invasion. I know, Dave—it ends when we leave.

We left via an unfamiliar road out of Falcon, varying our route to avoid the increasing number of IEDs set at the few choke points near the FOB's exits. Nobody wanted to be blown up ever, but being hit on your way home wasn't allowed to happen, except in bad war movies. This was a bad movie for sure, but not that ending this time. The area we transited outside the FOB was still a mess, a place where we dumped our garbage and sewage amid displaced Iraqis who lived off the picked-through refuse. Their homes were made of our discarded junk. The sewage puddles stood out as the only moisture, orange if chemical, gray-green if sewage, all eye-watering in the heat. Yet despite the filth, the kids still waved at our trucks, their bright clothing standing out from the monotone world around them, and the Army drivers would always wave back. The Iraqi adults never looked up. There was no value in their waving, for even gestures were saved for the work of picking a life out of whatever the Americans chose to leave for them.

Surprises lurked even in the familiar wasteland, and the driver marked my trip home by saying, "Sir, are those fucking horses?" We stopped for a moment, well against the regs, to stare at two horses walking slowly between puddles of shit. Two other horses lay in the muck, maybe cooling off as the temperature nudged past 100 degrees on this last morning in Iraq. We had seen many things in our time, but horses wandering this landscape were a first for us all. The gunner, on top in the turret, called for the 'terp to yell out to the old guy watching us. We learned that the swamp was once a horseracing track, built by Saddam and bombed away in all but the old guy's memory during the liberation in 2003. The horses had survived and now lived wild in the area, freedom at last brought by the Americans. The old guy told us there used to be more horses around, but what with urgent hunger in the worst of the postwar years, well, horses were what they had. It was a bad thing, the guy said, but the times were bad and nobody was happy about what bad times pushed you to do. We had stopped for too long, not safe, and the Truck Commander ordered us to drive on. The old man did not wave as we drove off.

The US had built Baghdad Airport back in the 1960s through some long-forgotten foreign-aid project that predated even Saddam. Now it was ours again; there was just too much irony around. The airport was part of a massive complex called Victory Base, bigger in land mass and in population than my hometown. Victory was a collection of subbases so numerous that I doubt anyone even knew the count anymore. The routing signs along the way offered some clue to where you were, telling you to turn left for the DynCorp compound, next right for retail gas, or directing you to "Ali's Hollywood," an Iraqi-run shop that sold illegal DVDs, porn if you asked the right way, and the iPod batteries that kept the war's soundtrack running. You saw a British flag on one compound, an Australian flag on another, likely small Special Forces enclaves, and lots of cryptically marked minifortresses the soldiers believed were encampments for our own Delta and SEALs—the whole menu of operators who kept the game alive.

Victory Base was so big that it had swallowed up what used to be islands in the archipelago of Saddam's palaces, dotted around the large lake that formed the center of the base. There were fish in the lake, big carp, and guys used to make poles and throw hooks in, baited with American cheese taken from lunch. Because of a rumor that Saddam used the lake as a dumping ground for his enemies' bodies, nobody actually ate the fish, fearing they had grown fat on Iraqi flesh. The Army expropriated all the palaces as offices for big shots, and even from the exteriors you could tell the interiors made Vegas look like Muji. The soldiers who drove me were eager tour guides, each with a more fantastic story to tell. Most of Saddam's palaces, they said as we drove, were part of an endless empire of whorehouses. One soldier insisted that Saddam was a pedophile and that a building we passed once held his harem of little boys. Another said no, that palace had been full of the female virgins Saddam enjoyed and had a tiger cage where those unwilling to give up their maidenhead were eaten alive (so the fish dined only on nonvirgins). Whether a tribute to US anti-Saddam propaganda or the imaginations of our troops, the stories made the long slog of a drive pass quickly, replacing the images of sad wild horses.

Every airport is purgatory, but BIAP—Baghdad International Airport—was one of the oddest places in-country. Most everywhere else folks were segregated, new guys from old guys, civilians from the Joes, that kind of thing. But BIAP was where all the wires crossed and you saw the inside of the war exposed. Everyone had to pass through the same set of doors to board something—a helo, a medevac, a C-130—to take them deeper into or farther from their war. You could tell by what people were wearing, new or old, and what they were carrying, a lot or almost nothing, who was coming in and who was already gone, gone, gone. A year ago I had passed through this place but I was damned if I could remember ever being here.

I was dropped off at the big central square where everyone waited outside the few buildings that constituted the terminal. I joined the troops already assembled in rows of chairs. They were watching soccer on a big TV, some unknown country versus another unknown country in a game they barely understood. But it was movement and that was close enough to entertainment, and when the team in green scored a goal the guys made themselves laugh by chanting, "USA! USA! USA!" The troops drank Rip Its and ate packaged donuts, looking deep into their twenties, trying to make BIAP feel like home, absent the warm beer and the high school girls, the fast food and the cars. So close to the exit, it was OK to allow yourself to think of those things again.

It was hot, really hot, and the heat accumulated around us one last time the same way snow would soon pile up back home. A lot of soldiers lay flat on the ground where they could find shade, heads propped on rucks, arms akimbo as their dreams got a head start on the flights to come. They were content if not comfortable, sprawled out on the ground with eyes closed and helmets off, but still it was a hard image to process when you'd seen the same thing bloody on roadsides. I shook my head; this was a place and time to start to let go, not to look back.

Waiting in line, we all agreed that the engineer who provided only four johns for the entire waiting area deserved to die upside down in one of them. Inside, at one of the basins, a soldier stood stripped to the waist, shaving. His face was well lathered and he was slowly moving the blue plastic razor over his chin and neck. His back was covered with angry scars, old scars, maybe from Iraq, maybe from a gang back home, but he had a stay-the-fuck-away-from-me aura and everyone gave him his distance. He made no eye contact, either with us or with himself in the mirror. Nobody broke the zone around him even though there were not enough sinks, and goddamn, did you want to wash your hands in this place.

Just before you entered the terminal from the waiting area there was a large cardboard box with a sign that asked you to donate unneeded toiletries for distribution to needy Iraqis. The box was empty and more than one guy looked at the sign and said "fuck that" as he walked past. The USO was giving away toiletries just nearby, single packs of tampons, minirolls of toilet paper, and three-ounce sticks of deodorant, so this was as absurd as anything else we'd seen on our tour.

We were all here, soldiers of every type, contractors, Southeast Asians waiting to be shipped to some distant FOB to wash dishes for us. The Asians looked scared, maybe in part because they were kitted with the oldest, cheapest body armor and helmets that seemed designed to not fit properly. We saw them as one group but the Sri Lankans couldn't talk to the Bangladeshis and only the Filipinos could speak any English anyway. I knew these people now: the contractors with Harley-Davidson

T-shirts, blue jeans, and big belt buckles, every man packing a set of keys like they were the superintendents of the war; the Embassy people, always easy to spot, in insanely out-of-place getups like white pants and Panama hats or in Banana Republic safari gear with big black GPS/calendar/videocam/chai-latte-making watches, $120 sunglasses, and freakish headgear like they were off to hunt elephant with Teddy Roosevelt. One of the Embassy guys had an American Tourister travel bag on his lap. American Tourister? I had flashes of the same man boarding a Pan Am flight back when you had to climb up those stairs on the outside of the plane, the stewardesses all wore miniskirts, and everybody drank gin and tonics. He was in the wrong war by about forty years.

Inside the terminal was another step toward home, cool and dark. Though most everyone was armed, we passed our bags through an X-ray anyway, manned in this case by a Ugandan contract security guard who could not be bothered even to look up at the monitor. He had mastered that Third World art of looking at nothing—safer that way, less likely to offend. We walked through the metal detector, every weapon and big Texas belt buckle making the buzzer scream. We kept our shoes on, unlike in any US airport, because everyone wore lace-up boots and it would have taken a hundred years to get them all on and off, and nobody was going to wait that long. In a rewind of my trip in, we got counted and recounted, our names on one clipboard, the last four digits of our social security number on another, and we recited our blood types for a long list of people who needed to record the information on yet more clipboards. No one complained about paying this price to move closer to the exit. The incomers didn't complain, because this was all new, and the outgoers knew complaining meant nothing but waiting another sentence to have to do it anyway. From time to time someone would appear and scream, "Chrome 18" or "Chrome 24," "chrome" being the code word for each flight. They could have said "Flight 18" or "18," but these people could have been nicer in many ways but preferred not to be. They never asked for respect, knowing none had been earned.

A lifetime later someone shouted "Chrome 19" and my leg twitched in memory that that was mine. "Chrome 19," not good-bye, or thanks, or anything else would be the last thing anyone would say to me in Iraq. We walked into the belly of a C-130, a cargo plane fitted with web seats. I was sandwiched between two equally sweaty people directly across from a tiny round window. Unlike everyone else aboard, who had only the noises of the engines and the vibrations below them to judge when the plane was moving, I could see out the window.

Airborne, the pilot dipped his right wing to turn and I saw the ground, Iraq, for the last time. I would be lying if I said I could see below me the wastelands I now knew were home to wild horses. I wanted to think I could make eye contact with one of the horses. She might look up and notice the plane overhead, the sun midway down the horizon, the smoke rising to the left where something had again gone terribly wrong in this sad place. She might have had in her thoughts the same vision that I held at that moment, colors that seemed to generate light, an image that, if the beast could think, she would have held in her mind forever. The horse had been there before I arrived, and I hoped she would go on a long, long time after I had left.

Notes

1. http://iraq-prt.usembassy.gov/20100804baghdad3.html.
2. Office of the White House Press Secretary, "Fact Sheet: Expanded Provincial Reconstruction Teams Speed the Transition to Self-Reliance," July 13, 2007.
3. http://iraq-prt.usembassy.gov/about-us.html.
4. http://thecable.foreignpolicy.com/posts/2010/08/18/chris_hill_s_farewell_tour.
5. http://michellemalkin.com/2007/11/07/a-diplomat-scolds-state-department-weenies/.
6. http://oig.state.gov/documents/organization/140420.pdf.
7. http://www.americanprogress.org/issues/2010/05/iraq_war_ledger.html.
8. http://news.yahoo.com/s/ap/20100728/ap_on_re_mi_ea/ml_iraq.
9. United States Government Accountability Office, *Iraqi–U.S. Cost-Sharing: Iraq Has a Cumulative Budget Surplus, Offering the Potential for Further Cost-Sharing*, September 2010.
10. MP 6743. MP and MG numbers refer to Department of State QRF projects.
11. TEC 103–6428.

12. Transparency International, *Corruption Perceptions Index 2010*, October 26, 2010.

13. Michael Schwartz, *War without End: The Iraq War in Context*, Haymarket Books, 2008.

14. Frederick Barton and Bathsheba Crocker, *Estimated Breakdown of Funding Flows for Iraq's Reconstruction: How Are the Funds Being Spent?* Center for Strategic and International Studies: Post-Conflict Reconstruction Project, December 2004, http://csis.org/files/media/csis/events/041201_iraq_funds.pdf.

15. Curt Tarnoff, *Iraq Reconstruction Assistance*, Congressional Research Service, March 12, 2009.

16. Brookings Institution, *Iraq Index: Tracking Variables of Reconstruction and Security in Post-Saddam Iraq*, http://www.brookings.edu/fp/saban/Iraq/index20060530.pdf.

17. *Rebuilding Iraq: Stabilization, Reconstruction, and Financing Challenges*, GAO Report to the Senate Foreign Relations Committee, GAO-06-428T, February 8, 2006, http://www.globalsecurity.org/military/library/report/gao/d06428t.pdf.

18. SIGIR, *Report to Congress*, April 30, 2007, http://www.sigir.mil.

19. SIGIR, *Report to Congress*, July 30, 2008, http://www.sigir.mil.

20. http://www.latimes.com/news/nationworld/world/la-fg-iraq-reconstruction-20100829,0,1409733,full.story.

21. Curt Tarnoff, *Iraq Reconstruction Assistance*, Congressional Research Service, March 12, 2009.

22. http://musingsoniraq.blogspot.com/2010/08/continued-problems-integrating-sons-of.html.

23. http://www.hrw.org/en/news/2010/04/27/iraq-detainees-describe-torture-secret-jail.

24. http://www.guardian.co.uk/world/2010/oct/22/iraq-detainee-abuse-torture-saddam.

25. http://www.stripes.com/article.asp?section=104&article=69339.

26. http://www.usf-iraq.com/?option=com_content&task=view&id=15315&Itemid=128.

27. http://article.nationalreview.com/349857/a-neighborhood-reborn/pete-hegseth.

28. http://www.cbn.com/cbnnews/310127.aspx.

29. http://www.army.mil/-news/2010/05/21/39590-local-art-show
-paints-bright-picture-for-iraqs-future/.
30. http://aidwatchers.com/2010/03/how-is-the-aid-industry-like-a
-piano-recital/.
31. http://www.npr.org/templates/story/story.php?storyId=129119290.
32. http://blogs.mcclatchydc.com/iraq/2010/04/great-news-for-soft
ball-and-baseball-iraqi-national-teams.html.
33. http://www.tac.usace.army.mil/deploymentcenter/tac_docs/GO
-1B%20Policy.pdf.
34. http://katieandchadwade.blogspot.com/.
35. MG 104–6465.
36. MP 133–7490.
37. MP 124–7279.
38. MG 112–6700.
39. MP 54–3936.
40. MP 38–2914.
41. MP 31–2458.
42. http://www.usf-iraq.com/?option=com_content&task=view&id=
28175&Itemid=128; http://www.facebook.com/note.php?note_id
=195401703528.
43. http://www.sigir.mil/files/audits/11-009.pdf#view=fit.
44. http://www.latimes.com/news/nationworld/world/la-fg-iraq-recon
struction-20100829,0,1409733,full.story.
45. http://www.doonesbury.com/strip/archive/2007/03/01.
46. http://www.hsus.org/animals_in_research/animals_in_research_
news/military_uses_pigs.html.
47. http://www.congress.org/news/2011/01/24/more_troops_lost_to_
suicide.
48. http://www.msnbc.msn.com/id/38267520.
49. http://www.brookings.edu/saban/iraq-index.aspx.
50. Andrew Bacevich, *Washington Rules: America's Path to Permanent War*,
Metropolitan Books, 2010, p. 86.
51. http://www.usip.org/files/file/resources/collections/histories/iraq_
prt/45.pdf, p. 2.
52. http://www.theatlantic.com/magazine/archive/2007/04/smoke-and
-mirrors/5849/.

53. http://www.latimes.com/news/nationworld/world/la-fg-iraq-recon struction-20100829,0,1409733,full.story.

54. http://www.au.af.mil/au/awc/awcgate/navy/art5-w98.htm.

55. http://ricks.foreignpolicy.com/posts/2010/05/06/.

56. http://www.fas.org/irp/doddir/army/fm3-24.pdf.

57. http://en.aswataliraq.info/?p=132514.

58. http://www.niqash.org/content.php?contentTypeID=28&id=2660 &lang=0.

59. http://www.sigir.mil/files/quarterlyreports/April2010/Report_-_ April_2010.pdf#view=fit.

60. http://www.reliefweb.int/rw/fullmaps_sa.nsf/luFullMap/ 41BA4475787A02B1852576470058C3FD/$File/map.pdf?.

Acknowledgments

Special thanks and more to my readers Lisa Ehrle, Mari Nakamura, Abby and Sarah Van Buren. Thanks also to Laurie Russo for the initial proofreading, Torie Partridge for the author photo, and to Raeka Safai for good counsel with a sense of humor.

My heartfelt gratitude to all the wonderful people at Metropolitan Books and the American Empire Project who worked to bring this story to daylight. In particular I am grateful to Sara Bershtel, Riva Hocherman, Steve Fraser, Tom Engelhardt, Jason Ng, and Roslyn Schloss.

Great thanks go to the men and women of the Third Brigade, 82nd Airborne Division, the First Brigade of the 3rd Infantry Division, and especially the Second Brigade of the 10th Mountain Division for their patience, time, and willingness to educate me during my year in Iraq. I came home safe because of your dedication and skill. Respect to my long-suffering Army S-9 partners Major Jason Conner, Major Geno Hwangbo, Captain Tom Eddy, and Mobile Max Ranger Minton, all good men who demonstrated professionalism while swimming upstream.

My thanks to Lieutenant Colonel Mike Davies and Lieutenant Colonel Mike Laabs, with whom I shared my fiftieth birthday, sipping whiskey from paper cups in the desert.

A shout-out to Deputy Assistant Secretary of State Robert Manazares, who helped inspire me.

Though we have never met or spoken, my thanks to *Dispatches* author Michael Herr. His book is required reading for anyone interested in modern conflict. Although presumptively about the Vietnam War, and while many sections speak about specific battles and places in Vietnam, his remains the best book ever written about the personal experience of being in war (*Catch-22* is in second place). *Dispatches* certainly informed my experience in Iraq, and every soldier I could persuade to read it came to the same conclusion. The chapter titles "Inhaling" and "Exhaling" are based on Herr's and appear in homage to his work.

Not thanks really but a special notice to Colin Powell and Condoleezza Rice, who led an organization I once cared deeply for into a swamp and abandoned us there. In a sad way, their actions created this book—I just wrote it all down. There was one little hint about how unimportant this all was to the highest levels of even the new management at State. On our last day of PRT training, the facility was put into lockdown for a visit from the new Secretary of State (it's cool that when she visits her own staff the Secretary's security puts us into lockdown). She greeted and congratulated the Afghan PRT class down the hall from us Iraqis, then left. We didn't even rate a walk-on. Our war no longer really mattered, though it would take me a long year in the desert and writing this book to fully figure that out.

About the Author

PETER VAN BUREN has served with the Foreign Service for over twenty-four years. He received a Meritorious Honor Award for assistance to Americans following the Hanshin earthquake in Kobe, a Superior Honor Award for helping an American rape victim in Japan, and another award for work in the tsunami relief efforts in Thailand. Previous assignments include Taiwan, Japan, Korea, the UK, and Hong Kong. He volunteered for Iraq service and was assigned to ePRT duty 2009–10. His tour extended past the withdrawal of the last combat troops.

Since the publication of this book, Van Buren's commentary has appeared in the *New York Times*, *Le Monde*, *The Guardian*, *The Huffington Post*, *Mother Jones*, *Foreign Policy*, TomDispatch.com and elsewhere. He has been a guest on NPR's *Fresh Air* and *All Things Considered* as well as *Democracy Now!* and has spoken at several major universities, the National Press Center, and to Army units deploying for Afghanistan.

Also since the publication of this book, the Department of State has begun termination proceedings against Van Buren, after reassigning him to a telework position and stripping him of his security clearance and diplomatic credentials.

Van Buren speaks Japanese, Mandarin Chinese, and some Korean. Born in New York City, he lives in Virginia with his spouse, two daughters, and a docile Rottweiler. This is his first book.

The American Empire Project

In an era of unprecedented military strength, leaders of the United States, the global hyperpower, have increasingly embraced imperial ambitions. How did this significant shift in purpose and policy come about? And what lies down the road?

The American Empire Project is a response to the changes that have occurred in America's strategic thinking as well as in its military and economic posture. Empire, long considered an offense against America's democratic heritage, now threatens to define the relationship between our country and the rest of the world. The American Empire Project publishes books that question this development, examine the origins of U.S. imperial aspirations, analyze their ramifications at home and abroad, and discuss alternatives to this dangerous trend.

The project was conceived by Tom Engelhardt and Steve Fraser, editors who are themselves historians and writers. Published by Metropolitan Books, an imprint of Henry Holt and Company, its titles include *Hegemony or Survival* and *Failed States* by Noam Chomsky, *The Blowback Trilogy* by Chalmers Johnson, *The Limits of Power* and *Washington Rules* by Andrew Bacevich, *Crusade* by James Carroll, *Blood and Oil* by Michael Klare, *Dilemmas of Domination* by Walden Bello, *Devil's Game* by Robert Dreyfuss, *A Question of Torture* by Alfred McCoy, *A People's History of American Empire* by Howard Zinn, *The Complex* by Nick Turse, and *Empire's Workshop* by Greg Grandin.

For more information about the American Empire Project and for a list of forthcoming titles, please visit www.americanempire project.com.